D1004185

INITIATIVE

INITIATIVE

A Rosicrucian Path of Leadership

TORIN M. FINSER, PH.D.

Lindisfarne Books
2011

2011
Lindisfarne Books
An imprint of Anthroposophic Press, Inc.
610 Main Street, Great Barrington, MA 01230
www.steinerbooks.org

LIBRARY OF CONGRESS CATALOGING-IN-PUBLICATION DATA

Finser, Torin M., 1956–
Initiative : a rosicrucian path of leadership / Torin M. Finser.
    p. cm.
Includes bibliographical references.
ISBN 978-0-88010-734-1
1. Business ethics. 2. Management—Moral and ethical aspects.
3. Leadership—Moral and ethical aspects. 4. Rosicrucians. I.
Title.
HF5387.F56 2011
658.4'092—dc22

2011010147

CONTENTS

This book is dedicated to my parents

Ruth and Siegfried Finser

for their encouragement, trust, and abiding love, which
have nourished me in more ways than I can measure.
They have my eternal gratitude.

ACKNOWLEDGMENTS

I would like to thank Jennifer Kershaw for her initial help with the first edits and Jens Jensen for pulling this project together. I thank my colleagues at Antioch University for providing a stimulating work environment that continually leads me to new questions, as well as the many members of the Anthroposophical Society in America who let me "try out" some of these topics in group meetings and conferences.

I would also like to thank my wife Karine Munk Finser for the cover image, which was originally designed for one of our Renewal Courses sponsored by the Center for Anthroposophy in Wilton, New Hampshire.

"*Be a person of initiative and beware, lest through hindrances of your own body or hindrances that otherwise come in your way, you do not find the center of your being, within which lies the source of your initiative. Observe that, in your life, all joy and sorrow, all happiness and pain, will depend on finding or not finding your own individual initiative.*" This should appear, as if written in golden letters, constantly before the soul of anthroposophists. Initiative lies in their karma, and much of what meets them in this life will depend on the extent to which they can become willingly, actively conscious of it.

—RUDOLF STEINER, August 4, 1924

INTRODUCTION

"HEAR ME GOD, I CAN'T TAKE IT ANYMORE . . ."

Leadership today is a modern Rosicrucian path of development. Those in positions of responsibility have to work with matter and the daily circumstances of the workplace. Yet in the face of the given realities of limited resources, they do their very best to manage people, the life forces of an organization, in such a way as to make progress. As will become more apparent further into this chapter, creating new value between the physical realities and the life-giving forces of human initiative is a modern Rosicrucian task.

Never has the challenge been greater. With acute financial pressures, many positions have been combined and people are having to do more with less. At times, it seems as if everything is measured by the bottom line, and yet leaders know how important it is to have motivated, spirited employees. How can life and matter coexist? How can we foster inner vitality in the face of mounting external pressures?

From August 4 to October 14, 2010, many of us followed the story of the thirty-three miners trapped deep underground in a mine in Chile. The story was riveting, not only in it's inherent human drama, but also in terms of unmistakable symbolism. Through the pneumatic tube-like devices the miners used to communicate, one of the miners wrote:

"I was born again at thirty-three years.... It is a coincidence, like a miracle, and for that, it gives me more strength to go forward." [1] Their call from deep in the earth was heard around the world, prompting donations and compassion from people regardless of nationality, race, or religion. This became one of those opportunities to experience the universal human, our "united-ness" as one people on this Earth. The cry that went straight into the hearts of people across the globe was the short phrase: "Hear me God, I can't take it anymore." [2]

What is it that humanity cannot take any more? It is the feeling of being trapped under many feet of matter. Imagine being in a cavern deep in the earth. Imagine the smells of coal dust, stagnant water, human perspiration and waste.... Then there is the emotional roller coaster of hope and despair, of hearing the doubts of others and the excruciating passage of time. To try and live with the existential question of life or death: rescue or not?

Then picture the gradual ascent in a capsule and the reemergence on Earth's surface. The indescribable joy of seeing one's loved ones again, the radiant sunshine, living plants and flowers, the splendor of the natural world. Imagine holding one's child and partner in a long embrace.

These two contrasting pictures are worthy of some soul space, not only in our compassionate carrying of those coal miners, but because of their educative value in themselves. We need to break out of our routine, our apathy of soul, or over-medicated inner life. The challenges of our time will not be overcome by conventional means. We need

---

1. *Wall Street Journal,* Oct. 8, 9, 2010, p. A10.
2. Ibid.

something really new, a spirited inner awakening. The suffering of the thirty-three coal miners gives us yet another invitation for such an awakening. This is beautiful.

The miles of earth above and around the miners was real in our normal sense of what constitutes reality. One could feel, touch, and measure it. Yet modern human beings are surrounded by a similar weight, though one that has a mirage quality, a shine that deludes us into thinking it is appealing. The weight of which I speak is materialism.

All around us we have people rushing to and fro, hurrying through their days, many in the pursuit of material things. Many people today work long hours with the hope of "rewarding" themselves with new gadgets, good food, cars, and vacations. These things have an apparent "shine," like sparkling images of light dancing on the surface of a lake. They sparkle, entice, and yet prove so fleeting that soon one has to get something else to satisfy the incessant craving.

Materialism haunts even some who are on a professed path of spiritual development: the fixation on the latest diet that results in counting what one eats and talking on and on about what one can and cannot consume, the so-called purchase of a private-school tuition for one's children, or buying self-help books with self-ambition in mind. There are many who have a "my family first" internal operating plan that can be ruthless when at a Little League game, or when standing in line at a children's fair and our dearest is shunted aside by a bully. Even if a person has managed to make progress with all of the above temptations of materialism, one has to also honestly assess one's thinking. Am I craving the food that I have declined, the money I am not earning? Materialism can live invisibly in our thoughts and feelings, and those are just as potent (if not more so) as the tangible objects many desire.

Above all, materialism eventually leads to a feeling of being trapped. It is like one of those escalators in an airport, the ones going up or down with masses of people and suitcases on them. It is very hard to get off once one is half way up or down.

The Rosicrucians did not deny matter (as was the case with many mystics). They did not attempt to flee the physical world, but instead they worked at the transformation that can come when life forces work in certain ways with material processes. They looked for that hidden element that lives between life and matter. Leaders today need to work with that third element, that space in-between, if they are to succeed. We need to develop a new science of leadership that calls upon cosmic, planetary wisdom, yet can work effectively on Earth in the here and now.

The first and third chapters of this publication are devoted to the questions raised in this introduction: living a spiritual life, Rosicrucian wisdom for today, and finding new resources for what I call planetary leadership.

Leaders today need to be people of initiative who are able to step forward, speak with purpose, and act with insightful courage. Where does initiative come from? How can leaders promote innovation in their organizations so we are not like little hamsters just running harder and faster on the wheels of life?

As is demonstrated in the second chapter, the question of initiative is intimately bound up with how we view the human being. How can we act out of freedom and in such a way that even with the most inspired initiative we still respect the freedom of the other? Where are we mistaken in our usual notions of freedom and how can Anthroposophy help us discover the inner conditions for freedom?

So, although the three chapters of this booklet started out as three separate speeches to three different audiences, they have a continuous thread: spirited leadership that can help transform the world.

It is my hope that the pages that follow will be used for discussion in groups as well as self-reflection and contemplation. After all, it is not the words themselves or the pages themselves that count (they, too, are simply more matter), but it is the work that ensues when readers take up the thoughts out of conscious intention. The inner work, depending on how it is done, can then lead to self-aware, living, insightful leadership prepared to perform new deeds of service.

Today we need to take that journey from the depths of the coal mine to the light of spirit day. Many people are doing this every day, and we need to join hands with these like-minded spirit seekers who have traveled up one mine shaft or another to emerge with new light of wisdom. Let us learn to recognize each other as spirit seekers. Let us see the eternal in each and every human being on this Earth.

LIVING A SPIRITUAL LIFE
IN AN AGE OF MATERIALISM

Living a spiritual life in our modern age is a challenge. Perhaps more than ever, contemporary trends seem to have conspired to hinder inner work. We need to look at the phenomena the world presents and identify some of the major themes as a first step in dealing with them. To know the world is essential to gaining knowledge of oneself.

Because of our recent financial crisis, many people around the world have had to acknowledge the false promise of materialism. For years, many people have responded to the temporary allure of bigger cars, houses, and other things of this world that provide superficial, transitory satisfaction. Yet much of this world of material acquisition was built upon false premises—derivatives, CDUs, SIVs are financial abstractions with little foundation in the real world. In today's world, as all of these objects of acquisition come crashing down, people have an opportunity to see the illusion behind our rampant materialism. Increasingly, I hear expressions of a longing for meaning, purpose, and fulfillment in life. Indeed, a spiritual reality is behind everything physical.[1]

A second contemporary trend is the ever more powerful role of the media, which plays upon fear and negativity and fosters inattention in a way that gradually stupefies and dulls our consciousness. The media throws gasoline

---

1. See Steiner, *An Outline of Esoteric Science,* pp. 119–120.

on the flames of issues such as the financial crisis, and a feeding frenzy results. Rather than enhancing conversation, electronic communications have actually helped isolate human beings as we sit in our chairs typing emails. The multi-billion-dollar collapse of the financial system and the extensive media coverage of finances of late present Ahriman with the perfect script to keep everyone's attention fixed as far away as possible from the Christ impulse. If one is continually tuned in to CNBC, it is hard to have any real thoughts of one's own.

Then we need to add the stress factor, the lack of rhythm in daily life as we rush from one thing to another. Some of us are so used to rushing that they do so even on a free day—stress has become a habit that leads to a host of physical ailments as well as frequent insomnia. We have become a restless society, bombarded with sensory stimuli with little time to process experiences.

Finally, one can observe gradual disconnections among the human soul forces; thinking, feeling, and willing no longer always work in harmony. How many of us have been in a meeting in which someone says something and then does the opposite afterward? Or, at other times, one feels there has been a real conversation that was "in-tune" with another person, only to hear a hurtful comment later on. In many cases, our thoughts, feelings, and deeds are not fully integrated, and this leads to further social fragmentation.

As we face all of the challenges of the day, there is a tremendous need to find wholeness and harmony again within the human soul, as well as reconnect with nature and the arts to counter modern stress. We need to see the universe in simple things and free ourselves from the subjectivity of the media. Rosicrucian Anthroposophy can help us with the modern challenges of materialism, disconnection, stress, and mass media through the pursuit of life-giving (etheric) forces that harmonize and unify. By being "present" with nature and by cultivating an active imagination through the arts, we can access ancient traditions that are more valuable today than ever before.

Let us start with prehistoric, pictorial consciousness and the tale of Briar Rose, told by many Waldorf schoolteachers. It is included here at some length not only because it will provide a resource for further discussion, but also because the very reading of it and living with the archetypal pictures can provide a source of nourishment for those seeking a spiritual life in our thorny modern world.

༃

The Tale of Briar Rose

A long time ago there were a king and queen who said every day, "Ah, if only we had a child!" But they never had one. However, it happened once that, as the queen was bathing, a frog crept out of the water onto the land and said to her, "Your wish shall be fulfilled. Before a year has gone by, you shall have a daughter."

The frog's prediction came about, and the queen had a little girl who was so pretty that the king could not contain himself for joy and ordered a great feast. He invited many kindred, friends, and acquaintances, as well as the wise women, so that they might be kind and well-disposed toward the child. There were thirteen of them in his kingdom. However, he had only twelve golden plates for them to eat from, so one of the wise women was not invited.

The feast was held with much splendor, and when it came to an end, the wise women bestowed their magic gifts upon the baby; one gave virtue, another beauty, a third riches, and so on, including everything in the world that one could desire.

When eleven of them had made their promises, suddenly the thirteenth entered. She wished to avenge herself for not having been invited and, without greeting or even looking at anyone, she cried with a loud voice, "The king's daughter shall in her fifteenth year prick herself with a spindle, and fall down dead." And without saying a word more, she turned and left the room.

They were all shocked, but the twelfth, whose good wish still remained unspoken, came forward. She could not undo the evil sentence but only soften it, so she said, "It shall not be death, but the princess shall fall into a deep hundred-year sleep."

The king, who would fain keep his dear child from the misfortune, gave orders that every spindle in the whole kingdom should be burned. Meanwhile, the gifts of the wise women were fulfilled in abundance on the young girl, for she was so beautiful, modest, good-natured, and wise that everyone who saw her was bound to love her.

It happened on the very day when the princess reached fifteen years of age that the king and queen were not at home, and the maiden was left in the palace quite alone. She went round the palace into all sorts of places, looked into rooms and bedchambers just as she pleased, and at last she came to an old tower. She climbed up the narrow, winding staircase and eventually reached a little door. A rusty key was in the lock, and when she turned it the door sprang open, and there in a little room sat an old women with a spindle, busily spinning her flax.

"Good day, old mother," said the King's daughter. "What are you doing here?"

"I am spinning," said the old woman, nodding her head.

"What sort of thing is that? It rattles round so merrily!" said the girl. With that, she took the spindle and wished to spin, too. But scarcely had she touched the spindle when the magic decree was fulfilled, and she pricked her finger with it.

At the very moment when she felt the prick, she fell upon the bed that stood there and lay in a deep sleep. Her sleep extended throughout the palace. The king and queen, who had just returned home and entered the great hall also began to sleep, and the whole of the court with them. The horses, too, went to sleep in the stable, as well as the dogs in the yard, the pigeons on the roof, and the flies on the wall. Even the fire flaming in the hearth became quiet and slept. The roasting meat left off sizzling, and the cook, who was just about to pull the hair of the scullery boy because he had forgotten something, let him go, and went to sleep. And the wind fell, and on the trees before the castle not a leaf moved.

Around the castle a hedge of thorns began to grow, and with every year became higher and eventually closed up round the castle and covered it, so that there was nothing of it to be seen, not even the flag upon the roof.

The story of the beautiful, sleeping "Briar Rose," for so the princess was named, went round the country, and from time to time the sons of kings would come and try to get through the thorny hedge and into the castle. However, they found it impossible, for the thorns held fast as if they had hands. Thus, the youths became caught in the thorn hedge and, unable to get loose, died miserable deaths.

After many long years, a king's son came to that country and heard an old man talking about the thorn hedge, and that it was rumored that behind the hedge stood a castle in which a wonderfully beautiful princess named Briar Rose had slept for a hundred years. The old man had heard, too, that the king and queen and the whole court were likewise asleep. He had heard from his grandfather that the sons of many kings had already come and had tried to get through the thorny hedge, but they had remained stuck fast in it and died pitifully.

Then the youth said, "I am not afraid; I will go and see the beautiful Briar Rose." The good old man tried to dissuade the young man, who would not listen to his words.

By this time, the hundred years had just passed, and the day had come when Briar Rose was to awake. When the king's son approached the thorn hedge, instead of thorns it bore large and beautiful flowers, which parted of their own accord to let him pass through unhurt and closed again behind him like a hedge.

In the castle yard, the young prince saw the horses and the spotted hounds lying asleep. On the roof sat the pigeons, asleep with their heads tucked under their wings. When he entered the house, the flies were asleep on the wall. The cook, asleep in the kitchen, was still holding out his hand to seize the boy, and the maid was sitting by the black hen, which she was about to pluck. As he continued into the great hall, he saw the entire court lying asleep, and up by the throne lay the king and queen.

The prince went on farther, and it was so quiet that a breath could be heard, and finally he came to the tower, and he opened the door to the little room where Briar Rose was sleeping.

There she lay, so beautiful that he could not turn his eyes away, and he stooped down and gave her a kiss. Just as soon as he kissed her, Briar Rose awoke, opened her eyes, and looked at him quite sweetly.

The youth and Briar Rose then went down together. The king and queen then awoke, along with the whole court, looking at one another in great astonishment. The horses in the courtyard stood up and shook themselves, and the hounds jumped up and wagged their tails. The pigeons on the roof pulled their heads from under their wings, looked round, and flew into the open country. The flies on the wall began to crawl about again, the fire in the kitchen flamed up, flickered, and began cooking the meat, which began to turn and sizzle again. Now the cook gave the boy such a knock on the arm that he screamed, and the maid finished plucking the fowl.

Now the marriage of the prince with Briar Rose was celebrated with great splendor, and they all lived contented to the end of their days.[2]

∿

---

2. *Grimm's Fairy Tales*, pp. 237–241 (trans. revised).

Here we have in a simple fairy tale two pictures that speak with untold wisdom. First came the longing for a child, then the joy of birth, and then the sons of kings who became entangled in the thorns and lost their lives.

Birth and death are the two portals of a lifespan. The physical body cannot exist alone, but requires life forces, or "etheric forces" in Rudolf Steiner's term. The Rosicrucians were fascinated by the boundaries, the in-between places of matter and life, birth, and death. They sought what lives between the physical and the etheric, a substance more precious than gold.

> It is a substance that is contained in every other physical substance, so that the other physical substances can be considered to be modifications of this one substance. To see this substance clairvoyantly was the endeavor of the Rosicrucians. The preparation, the development of such vision they recognized as requiring a heightened activity of the soul's moral forces, which would then enable them to see this substance. They realized that the power for this vision lay in the moral power of the soul.[3]

They found this substance. It was present both in the macrocosm of the world at large and in the individual human being as a kind of garment that arose in the harmonious interplay of thinking and willing. They saw the will forces not only in humans but also in all of nature, in thunder and lightning, tree and stone. And they saw thought not only present in the human being but in the rainbow and the early shimmering of dawn. Thought and

---

3. Steiner, *Christian Rosenkreutz*, p. 21.

will live in the world around us, and when there is harmony between the two, in the world and in us, we have the possibility for moral forces that give health and well being.

Thus, the Rosicrucian mystery wisdom and the story of Briar Rose address one of the key challenges of our time as identified earlier—the fragmentation of human soul forces. The heart can open only when the head and the will work together in harmony. Yet there is still more to be gleaned from our story.

First, the twelve wise women gave their gifts to the child, an early rendition perhaps of the twelve wise teachers who shared their wisdom with Christian Rosenkreutz during an early incarnation. The gifts represent the accumulated wisdom of humankind, but even that cannot replace individual destiny.

The thirteenth gift and pricking the finger on the spindle is a particularly difficult mystery picture. A clue may be found in something that is left unsaid but implied; anyone who has suffered a serious injury knows how one's blood can flow from even the smallest injury. With the image of blood, we see that the human individuality is at stake, the "I," the inner self that is prepared during adolescence.[4] The loss of childhood and the birth of a new sense of self is a crucial rite of passage, not just for teenagers, but also for the threshold experiences of the spirit seeker. Living a spiritual life today requires the pricking of conscience, causing us to awake from the spell of our deep sleep.

---

4. The accompanying piece on freedom and initiative goes into more detail on the mysterious, twofold aspect of the human "I."

Moreover, not only the maiden, but also the entire castle is surrounded by a hedge of thorns that envelops everyone in a bubble of sleep for a hundred years. Again, we know that a hundred years is a very special period; it regularly marks the repeated rebirths of Rosicrucian wisdom in each century.[5] This period is a kind of earthly silence, a time that is free of vain pride and ambition. The hundred-year growth of the hedge of thorns also served as a kind of protection from outer attacks of an astral, emotional nature, which would hinder the gradual strengthening of the etheric forces. Likewise, the being of Christian Rosenkreutz was able to grow stronger with the passage of each century, to the point where he could be effective even without a new physical body.[6]

Finally, and not be overlooked, the king's son was able to awaken Briar Rose at exactly the right time, when the hundred years had come to an end. In our modern world, there are few who still have a sense for what the Greeks called *kairos,* the right time to do something. Despite the many modern devices that create synthetic environments, human health and wellbeing still call for the appropriate amount of waking and sleeping, speaking and remaining silent. *Kairos* is an antidote to the media frenzy mentioned in the introduction. Instead of externally induced sensory bombardment, the spiritually aware human being can set the clock through the life forces of rhythm and discernment for the right place and time.

What happens during sleep? The story of Briar Rose goes to great lengths to emphasize how *everything* was

5. Steiner, *Christian Rosenkreutz,* p. 21.
6. Ibid., p. 23.

sleeping. We each spend as much as a third of our lives asleep (even during lectures). Years ago, when doing research for my doctorate, I did a survey of public and Waldorf schoolteachers and asked them when they do most of their preparation. As expected, they did it in the evening before sleep. Then I asked when they receive most of their inspirations, the "aha" moments that transform a good lesson into an excellent lesson, and sixty-six percent of the public schoolteachers and seventy-one percent of the Waldorf teachers said they received their inspirations in the morning upon waking and emerging from sleep. How interesting. Something significant must happen during sleep.

We know from research at the Dartmouth Hitchcock Sleep Center in New Hampshire and other studies that sleep is a time to process the day's experiences. Rudolf Steiner goes further to describe in some detail the journey during sleep. We not only "digest" the events of the day, but we also *gather resources for living.* We encounter the hierarchies and meet our guiding *genius,* as represented in this verse:

> I go to sleep
> Till I awaken
> My soul will be in the spiritual world,
> And will there meet the higher Being
> Who guides me through this earthly life—
> Him who is ever in the spiritual world,
> Who hovers about my head.
> My soul will meet him,
> Even the guiding Genius of my life.
> And when I waken again
> This meeting will have been.

I shall have felt the wafting of his wings.
The wings of my Genius
Will have touched my soul.[7]

We will see the importance of sleep again in an even more mysterious text, *The Chymical Wedding of Christian Rosenkreutz,* but first let us look more closely at that hedge of thorns.

We know from our work with Anthroposophy that growth is an expression of etheric forces, and that light is needed for a hedge to grow. When light is accepted by a plant, it can be transformed into living substance. What lives in plants uses light to produce life.

For growth to occur, however, one also needs earthly substances—magnesium, water, potassium, and carbon dioxide. The invisible meets the visible in the plant world. The Rosicrucians were very interested in exploring what exists behind matter, as well as the boundary between physical and etheric substances. They felt, too, that if the human soul could develop greater moral strength it would be possible to see beyond the usual *maya* of matter.

"The etheric body is a body of harmony.... We are formed by a harmony that comes from a higher world.... The construction of our etheric body is crystallized religion, is harmony."[8] We have only to look at some of the great cathedrals (Chartres, for example) to see the laws of harmony at work in architecture. Life forces worked through human beings in such artistic creations. We can also apply what we know of the etheric to human thinking, even though, as Dr. Wolff says, "Thinking is

7. Finser, *School Renewal,* p. 100.
8. Wolff, *The Etheric Body,* p. 6.

a complicated action, so much so that many people are afraid to do it." [9]

What happens when we think? We need some direction and focus, which comes from the "I." We also have to be awake, of course (the astral needs to be present). However, the basis of thinking, the substance with which we think, is comprised of transformed etheric forces. Just try to think clearly when you are very tired, when your life forces are ebbing; it is much more difficult. Once we have rested, our thinking is again supported. So we can say that in thinking we transform life into ideas.

This is the basis of Rosicrucianism; the extensive study of earth, air, fire, and water, as well as the special fifth element, the etheric. The Rosicrucians were very interested in how the "freed" life forces can be taken into human thinking. Self-directed, transformative thinking can harmonize and reconnect spirit and matter. When this occurs, the Prince "for whom the hedge of thorns parts" is present with the power of clear thinking, and the sleeping soul is awakened so that there can be unity again as represented in the marriage of Briar Rose and the king's son.

In the union of the two we have the possibility of giving birth to new life. Rosicrucian training has made it possible that in modern times we can develop the etheric so far that it can actually work exoterically. Life forces can be visibly formative in the physical world around us, if we but have the eyes to see.

This provides an interesting context for the experience of Paul on the road to Damascus. He was suddenly able to behold something he had not been able to see before. Indeed,

---

9. Ibid., p. 11.

"it is the work of the Rosicrucians that makes possible the etheric vision of Christ."[10] To live a spiritual life in our modern age is to become more and more like Paul, seeing beyond the usual sensory-bound world.

This means being able to look through, forge through, and then pass through the "thickets" we often encounter in life—not just as in the Briar Rose story told earlier. Those thickets can be interpersonal, organizational, or psychological, but they have the common purpose of waking us up. Thorns, those sharp, earthy, pointed structures that can so easily cause injury were used to crown the head of Christ on the way to Golgatha. As he took that painful journey, his head began to bleed, and his life forces began to dissipate. The head is, in many ways, the most dense, earth-bound part of our body. The crown of thorns and the flowing blood represent the process of transformation in its early stages. Through the difficulties we face in life, we have a chance to grow more conscious, awake to new dimensions, and experience moments of resurrection.

We can say that, when the gravity of materialism takes over, we are covered in thorns. How great it is when we can nevertheless see one another despite the thorns. Rumi put words to this experience in his love poem:

> O Sweet Bitterness!
> I will soothe you and heal you
> I will bring you roses
> I, too, have been covered with thorns.[11]

Thus, Rumi describes how his beloved receives him despite arriving home covered in thorns—she brings him roses.

---

10. Steiner, *Christian Rosenkreutz*, p. 23
11. Chopra, *The Love Poems of Rumi*, p. 27.

The Rosicrucians were intent on preparing the resurrection body. Overcoming the thorns is to find redemption in Christ.

Let us now turn to an esoteric parable, the well-known *Chymical Wedding of Christian Rosenkreutz*. There is much to this amazing story, but I have chosen a few key imaginations that have particular bearing on the theme of living a spiritual life in our modern world. I dedicate this discussion to the consummate master teacher of history, Henry Barnes, who taught with such vivid imagination that his stories and images have remained with me for decades.

In regard to *The Chymical Wedding*, we begin with four pathways. After receiving an invitation to the wedding, the main character, Christian Rosenkreutz, undertakes a long journey. Along the way, he is presented with a choice of four possible routes.

The first is short but dangerous. There are rocky places, and treacherous terrain that can be extremely hazardous.

The second way is longer but easier to travel. However, one has to be very careful not to veer to the right or left. For the sake of safety, it is essential to stay on the straight and true way.

The third is the royal way, with its many pleasures and pageants that can tempt and distract.

The fourth is a consuming way; it is, in a practical sense, only for incorruptible bodies. One has to have achieved a high degree of perfection to go the fourth way.[12]

---

12. Pfeiffer, *The Chymical Wedding of Christian Rosenkreutz*, p. 11.

Our traveler Christian Rosenkreutz cannot decide which path to choose, especially because the instructions state that, once on a path, turning back may lead to death. While considering his path, Rosenkreutz shares his food with a dove that is then attacked by a raven. The poor dove is frightened and the raven chases it. Our friend runs after them to help the dove. He succeeds in driving off the raven only to find that he has inadvertently chosen one of the four pathways and now cannot turn back because of a strong wind.

Here, in pictorial form, is a truly modern situation. Which pathway should I take? How do I navigate relationship? Those who are younger may ask: What is my vocation? Those in the middle years of life may ask: Should I make a change in the path I have followed thus far? We have choices to make, even in the later years of life.

The short but rocky path is like the physical body, whose time is short on Earth. The second, longer way involves the etheric, which prefers steady rhythm and whose boundaries must be honored. The third path is one of being conscious of both pleasure and pain. It is a way of potential distractions on a soul level. And finally, self-directed transformation can lead to a higher level of being, whereby one works through the "I" and possibly follows the fourth path. We have not only four roads, but also a complete picture of the human being as physical, etheric, astral, and "I."

Our traveler Christian Rosenkreutz is drawn out of his dilemma with the arrival of the dove and the raven—the raven a classic sign of warning, the dove a bringer of hope and rebirth. By following the dove, our traveler finds his way, providing a wonderful picture of following the winged spirit in one's journey through life. Is our compassion strong enough to help those in need and lead us to rebirth?

Another interesting aspect of the *Chymical Wedding* is the entrance to the towers, which requires a gift in exchange for a token of welcome as a Brother of the Rose Cross. Our traveler hands over some salt, then water, and he eventually witnesses flames on the ships at night. These are the ancient alchemical elements of salt, mercury, and sulfur at work.

In nature, a deposit of salt was seen as a call for a corresponding soul process. Salt for the Rosicrucians was seen as the tendency to destroy human nature through instincts and passions. The salt process represents decomposition, even putrefaction, when we blindly follow our instincts. To counter this, Rosicrucians felt a need to develop "noble thoughts that turn toward the spirit."[13]

As human beings, we need to bring our thoughts to a higher level of development, which can lead to greater health in our next life. Remaining with our instincts, on the other hand, can eventually lead to illness. Try, for example, watching an hour of television from this point of view, observing the struggle between noble thoughts and appeals to our instincts.

In contrast to salt, mercury is a substance that dissolves, just as water tends to renounce form. The corresponding soul process is love. Combustion, a sulfur process, indicates a soul quality of devotion to the divine, a deep religious feeling that can be kindled by a work of art, a poem, or a moving experience.

---

13. Steiner, *Esoteric Christianity,* p. 61.

Thus, we may ask: *How can we integrate the three processes described here into daily life?* How can we cultivate noble thoughts, love, and devotion in our modern world? We need to begin viewing everything around us as imbued with spiritual qualities. For instance, copper is not just a metal; spiritually, it can also signify divine thoughts. Silver contains ancient wisdom that speaks of love, while gold represents devotion and divine sacrifice.[14] Everything physical is an expression of spirit. We need to *know* this and carry it in our everyday consciousness; then we will truly begin to practice stewardship of our Earth, which is our calling today.

We cannot leave the *Chymical Wedding* without discussing the number seven. A rope is lowered into the dungeon seven times. On the third day the visitors are weighed on scales with seven weights. Seven coffins are placed in seven ships at the end of the fourth day. And there are seven round towers on the fifth day. The number seven appears numerous times in this esoteric parable. What does it mean?

The Rosicrucians spoke of two components of seven—three and four. Groups of three were connected especially to the spiritual world, the secrets of the stars, and they expressed their wisdom in symbols. Groups of four brought their wisdom directly to the people through fairy tales and legends, such as the story of Briar Rose and the *Chymical Wedding*. The two groups depend on each other. Without the group of three, "fours" would have had no

---

14. This theme of metals and cosmic influences will reappear in the chapter on planetary leadership.

content. Without the fours, the "threes" would have been able only to stammer to the world.[15]

The smaller group of three works with the esoteric content but needs the others to help it find expression in the world. The larger group of four needs the fountainhead of the "three" for sustenance. Even today we have this reciprocity in the relationship between the School for Spiritual Science and the General Anthroposophical Society, the smaller and larger circles that share a common home at the Goetheanum in Dornach, Switzerland.

Along the journey to the *Chymical Wedding,* our traveler meets many seals and inscriptions, one of which reads:

AR.NAT.MI. Art is the priestess of Nature

Indeed, the anthroposophic movement differentiates itself from others "precisely through the will to be connected to the arts."[16] Through the arts, Earth becomes spiritualized, and the human "I" is able to incarnate more fully. The act of artistic creation, whether through music, painting, drama, or another form, is a Rosicrucian deed for our time. It is the transformation of substance through human efforts. Human soul forces are reconnected as the *will* moves through *feeling* and into *thinking* itself. Rather than withdraw from the physical world (as was the tendency with some Theosophists), Rosicrucian Anthroposophists enter nature and worldly affairs so that Earth can be transformed.

---

15. Schmidt-Brabant and Sease, *Paths of the Christian Mysteries,* p. 170.
16. Ibid.

We are not alone in this work. I was deeply moved as I read several accounts of Paul Newman's life, and I wish to honor him by including a few of his last words that describe his philanthropy, camps for ailing children, and other endeavors: "We are such spendthrifts with our lives. The trick of living is to slip on and off the planet with the least fuss you can muster. I'm not advocating anyone for sainthood; I just happen to think that in life we need to be a little like the farmer who returns to the soil everything that is taken from it." [17] In Paul Newman we had a modern-day Rosicrucian, as shown by his acting, his philanthropy, and his attitude toward life.

Having mentioned both Henry Barnes and Paul Newman, I need to close this section with one more great spirit who now works with us from across the threshold. Just a few short months before his passing, I visited William Ward, a beloved, longtime teacher at Hawthorne Valley School in Ghent, New York. He struggled for more than two years with the type of brain cancer that also afflicted Senator Ted Kennedy.

With halting speech and eloquent gesture, William shared several gems with me. For example, creating a small place with his hands and then reaching out into an expansive gesture William said, "The ordinary things we concern ourselves with everyday are so small, yet the spiritual worlds are so, so vast." With his joy and optimism, even when suffering, and with his abiding faith in the human spirit, William continued to produce amazing pageants at the Hawthorne Valley School.

---

17. *New York Times,* Sept. 28, 2008, p. 26.

William Ward placed one of his favorite Novalis poems in his book *Traveling Light*.

> The heart is the key to life and the world.
> If our life is as precarious as it is,
>   it is so only that we should love and need one another.
> Because of the fact that we are each of us insufficient, we
> Become open to the intervention of another, and it is this
>   intervention which is the goal.
> When we are ill, others must look after us;
>   and only they can do so.
> From this point of view,
> Christ is indisputably the key to the world. [18]

So with William Ward, Paul Newman, and Henry Barnes working with us from across the threshold, I would like to dedicate the years ahead to working with renewed Rosicrucian wisdom.

> Let us be fully "present" in the natural world, seeing
>   Nature as the fount of life forces, the second way as
>   portrayed in the Chemical Wedding.
> May we see each other through the hedge of thorns and
>   find the roses, the transformation of rebirth.
> Let us enliven our thinking so that we take the light of
>   consciousness and see beyond the veil of materialism
>   and the media.
> May the "priestess of nature," Art, live ever more strongly
>   in our work.
> Finally, let us reach out to the guidance of Christian
>   Rosenkreutz who has sacrificed himself to remain with
>   us in these times when we need him most.
> Working together toward these goals, we can truly live a
>   spiritual life despite the challenges of our modern time.

---

18. Ward, *Traveling Light,* p. 17.

FREEDOM
AND INITIATIVE

Can an individual human being still make a difference today? All of us have lived a significant part of our lives in the twentieth century. Yet as we look back, despite tremendous technological and material progress, the last hundred years have done little to resolve some of the most fundamental issues facing humanity. Despite wars and even revolutions fought in the name of freedom, few people today are truly free, or even have a real conception of freedom. As for taking initiative, many feel hobbled by organizational structures, financial constraints, and the general hectic pace of our modern lives. Yet as I hope to demonstrate, freedom and initiative go to the very heart of our human condition, and provide those who work with Anthroposophy a special opportunity to respond to the needs of the world today.

Along the way, I would like to introduce you to a new friend of mine, as well as mention three of the ghosts that still haunt us from the past century. Finally, I hope to share a few thoughts on how the Anthroposophical Society might even more fully realize its mission in the twenty-first century.

Freedom

In *Goethe's Theory of Knowledge,* Rudolf Steiner states, "Our philosophy is a philosophy of freedom, therefore, in the highest sense.... The free human spirit acts according to its own insight, without the intrusion of any kind of compulsion—*according to self-determined commands."* [1] The opening question for us is therefore: On what basis do we arrive at insights that allow such self-directed, free decisions?

I would like to begin with the assertion that freedom is an inner condition that rests upon a fertile bed of soul conditions that supports the true intentions of the human spirit. Any exploration of freedom needs to look at these soul conditions and the inner resources needed—indeed all of Anthroposophy is dedicated to helping the striving human being create and nurture the inner conditions that make freedom possible. To start, let us look at the notion of impartiality in everyday life.

To accomplish this, we need to find a balance between opening our senses to the rich world of impressions around us and at the same time rejecting any sort of compulsion, whether external or internal. We want to be open to the beauty of the natural world, such as the wonderful colors we find in flowers during the summer months, while at the same time protecting our senses from the onslaught that comes from the media and advertising. This battle of the senses, fought on a daily basis, is one threat to our freedom. Another, far more subtle threat is the one-sided prejudices that can come

1.   Steiner, *Goethe's Theory of Knowledge,* pp. 91–92.

from deeply held inner convictions. How often do we see others through lenses we choose to wear?

During a recent trip to China, I was surprised at myself. Only when I was there did I see how varied the people are, depending on the province they come from or their family background. Prior to that time, I had carried one predominant visual image of an abstract Chinese person. How many unexamined and, therefore, unintended prejudices do we all carry with us?

When speaking of impartiality, Rudolf Steiner said, "Freedom means not only that I am free from the compulsion of an outer authority, but above all that I am not subservient to my own prejudices, opinions, sensations, and feelings." [2] Even with the advice of esoteric teaching, one cannot allow blind acceptance of an external authority. Rather, we become free through *practicing* sound advice and making it our own. Therefore, although there are different spiritual paths, whether Eastern traditions or Christian, it is a particular aspect of the Rosicrucian approach that it involves nothing at all contrary to modern humankind's sense of freedom.

In taking the notion of impartiality a step further, we can say that, on a daily basis, we tend to know the life of the soul from one side. Because we are immersed in it, we tend to see the world from within outward. I am here, and the world is around me out there. This tends to allow us to see only the surface of things, and the danger (as just described) is that we either view the world too much through our own lenses, or we let the external sensory world rule the impressions we take into our soul life.

---

2.   Steiner, *The Stages of Higher Knowledge*, p. 17.

However, there is another step that seekers of freedom can take. Instead of looking at the external world from the outside and experiencing ourselves from inside, as seekers we can "'slip out of our skin,' as it were, to observe ourselves from outside. This objective observation of *our self* is literally our first obligation in esoteric training." [3] This is a crucial step toward attaining greater freedom.

This stepping outside of ourselves is a radical reconstruction of our day-to-day self-experience. We tend to go around with a somewhat vague feeling that "I am in myself," meaning that somewhere in this physical body is a point of reference. Our entire material culture is built around satisfying the needs (and wants) of the physical body as pretext for serving the Self. "Give yourself a break today" was McDonald's tagline for many years, implying that your "self" could be met and satisfied by a deluxe hamburger.

Similarly, in our daily interactions with one another, we tend to see separate unities, I am here, you are there. In reading *Theosophy*, one can come away with the concept that the "I" is the kernel of the soul. This common understanding of our "I" is an illusion we need for living in our sense-bound world. However, in the admonition "Know thyself and know the world; Know the world and know thyself" is a hint of something more. The revelation of the world within the physical body entails the earthly "I," or Self. The usual understanding of the "I" is a projection of my self into my body. Yet anyone who has worked with young children knows that, in their wonderful powers of imitation, something else is also at work, something that

3.   Steiner, *The Stages of Higher Knowledge,* p. 30.

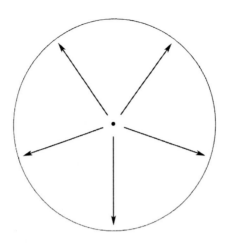

works inward from the periphery. Know the world and know yourself.

In a lecture in 1911, "The Psychological Basis of Spiritual Science," Rudolf Steiner describes the transcendent "I" that uses the physical body as a kind of mirror of consciousness: "The 'I' is not *in* the body but outside.... One's physical activity represents only a living mirror that reflects the life of the 'I' within the transcendental." [4] Just as Goethe said that "the light creates the eye so the eye can observe the light," [5] so it is that one's "I" needs the physical to observe its reflected image and become aware. As human beings, we need to distinguish between the reflected image of the "I" embedded in our everyday experience of our physical existence and the *true* reality of the "I," which is free of such constraints, free of the everyday concerns that so often occupy our consciousness.

4. Steiner, "The Psychological Basis of Spiritual Science," lecture in Bologna, March 1911.
5. Goethe, *The Theory of Colors*, p. liii.

Anthroposophy gives us this crossing point, the path of freedom, in which the "I" is transcendent and the body is physical. We, through conscious intention, can move between the everyday "I" and the transcendent "I."

Another way to describe this can be found in Arthur Zajonc's book *Meditation as Contemplative Inquiry,* in which he differentiates between the social self, the common "I," and the silent self, the not-"I."[6] In Buddhism, this is described as the "no-self," or *an-atman,* and in Christianity, as St. Paul's "not I but Christ in me." In all cases, our attention moves from the center to the periphery, from everyday concerns to the transcendent and eternal.

> I am not I.
> I am this one
> Walking beside me whom I do not see,
> Whom at times I manage to visit,
> And whom at other times I forget;
> The one who remains silent when I talk,
> The one who forgives, sweet, when I hate,
> The one who takes a walk when I am not,
> The one who will remain standing when I die.[7]

This poem by Ramon Jimenez describes beautifully the relationship between these two aspects that journey with us through life and even through the portal of death. The following verse by Rudolf Steiner further describes this particular relationship that lives beyond the portal of death:

> I gaze into the darkness
> In it arises Light —

6. Zajonc, *Meditation as Contemplative Inquiry,* p. 31.
7. Ibid.

Living Light.
Who is this Light within the darkness?
It is I myself in my reality.
This reality of the "I"
Enters not into my earthly life;
I am but a picture of it.
But I shall find it again
When, with good will for the Spirit,
I have passed through the gate of death.[8]

Early during the summer of 2010, my daughter Louisa graduated from the twelfth grade at High Mowing School, our fifth child to do so (we have one more to go). Two weeks later, one of her classmates of twelve years was killed in a car accident. In her yearbook, her friend had drawn a picture of herself as a young child playing on Earth. Above the child, she drew the Sun large with some clouds. Above the clouds was another picture of the same child, this time with wings as she looked down to Earth. At the very bottom of the picture were the words, "I can't know where I'm going without knowing where I've been." And one more detail: in the center of the large, yellow Sun were the simple words, "Thank you."

Thus, in addition to the path of conscious self-development described in Anthroposophy, which can help train the development of capacities for a new state of freedom concerning the "I" and self, life also offers unexpected opportunities to work with "awakening" moments. These moments include illnesses. Increasingly, people experience and express the fact that their lives were unfulfilled until illness became a wise teacher. Many of the stories of illness point to the transcendent "I."

8. Steiner, *Verses and Meditations*, p. 197.

There are also other occurrences of crises, earthquakes, and the like that can lead to spirit awakening. Especially in times of economic challenge, many people today feel the old material supports slipping away and, through self-observation, sense that life is calling for a new beginning. When realized, whether through the portal of death, an illness, or economic struggle, people are prompted to observe themselves. Although they may not use such terms as "transcendent I," the activity itself is liberating. The result is more self-aware action, the bedrock of human freedom.

Here it is worthwhile to say a few words about freedom and those involved in spiritual movements such as Anthroposophy. This is the first of the three ghosts I hinted at earlier. It is ironic, perhaps, though I hope not inevitable, that those who have achieved a sort of spiritual certainty in their lives can *inadvertently restrict the freedom of others.*

If I understood correctly, our friends in Holland who interviewed people who were leaving the Anthroposophical Society reported that some said they were leaving because they wanted to reclaim their freedom. How could this be, when the very core of Anthroposophy is the notion of freedom? I took this remark (if accurate) to reflect a human failing, not a shortcoming in Anthroposophy. It is a challenge to all who are inspired, who have found certain truths, that we tend to advocate for those selfsame truths without always inquiring enough about the other person. If I am certain about something, does this give me license to expound and explain regardless of the human condition represented in the person across from me? In the name of freedom, we may want to remind ourselves that there is value in entertaining questions together, while avoiding leaps to conceptual formulations of answers. A student once said of a teacher, "He answered all the questions I never knew I had." This can be stimulating, but can also verge on dogmatism. Are we willing to live occasionally with ambiguities? Are we willing to live with multiple perspectives?

The image of the caravan traveling east, with a long train of camels, wagons, and pilgrims, has inspired many who work with the notion of "servant leadership." At the far end of the procession, surrounded in the dust and tumult, is the small figure of a man helping and supporting those in need. As told by Hermann Hesse in *Journey to the East,* it later turns out that the inconsequential pedestrian was in fact a leader of a high spiritual order. This image has often inspired me in my work. Can we come to be known less for all the things we can say, the lectures we reluctantly learn to give, and more for our service? Accompanying someone on the trail, walking in the dust if need be, connects us with the rhythmic pulse and heartbeat of humanity.

When we take interest in the other, walk in someone else's moccasins, we can live into the world as experienced by the other. After walking some way down the trail together, we can then offer help in a grounded context, truly respectful of the other's individuality. In this way, we do not impose, but serve. In this way, spiritual truths are revealed in the right time rather than expounded rhetorically. Living in the "presence of the other" is to live in relationship, cultivating the space "in-between," which contains the possibility for freedom.

To summarize, let us be known not just by how we explain freedom, but by how we exercise it in our work with fellow human beings.

Initiative

Just as the human soul is the starting point for reclaiming freedom, it also is the basis for fostering initiative as a way forward in the twenty-first century. While these considerations of freedom have much to do with imaginative consciousness, the next section on initiative will have to do with accessing inspiration and intuition as resources for active deeds on Earth. Just as we need to transform our imagination in picturing the "I" and the self, we need a new way of working with feelings and willing so that we can support a culture of entrepreneurship and innovation.

One exercise involves working with what is "true" and, in tandem, working with what is "false." We allow the juxtaposition of the true alongside the false to work repeatedly to gradually develop a heightened faculty of judgment. Not only do we become more sensitive to an erroneous opinion, even to the degree of experiencing an error as inner pain, but we must also develop tolerance toward the very person expressing such an erroneous view. With time, this inner struggle can produce "quick-witted judgment and unerring certainty of decision."[9] Thus, one learns to act and decide more effectively when such exercises have been carried for a while.

Ancient Chinese medicine teaches us that each act should consume only the amount of energy needed for

---

9. Steiner, *The Stages of Higher Knowledge*, p. 36.

that deed, no more, no less. We often become tired simply because we exert too much energy for tasks that could be done with less. This conservation of human life forces (*qi*) can be considered also from the point of view of the human soul. Emotions such as fear or anxiety also entail an expenditure of soul force. One could say that soul force is lost when one gives way to fear and anxiety. But if one can curtail the emotion, such as fear, the soul force remains available for other purposes. "If we repeat such processes often, we build up an inner treasure of these continually husbanded soul forces, and we soon find that, out of such economies of feeling, arise the germs of those inner images that bring to expression the revelations of a higher life."[10]

Thus, if during the course of normal living one practices this exercise of exposing oneself to events while denying the emotional gratification of simply going with the flow of feelings, gradually an inner resilience is developed that becomes the fertile ground for inspirations. Rather than making us cold and without feeling, this exercising of the soul produces a kind of receptivity to higher forces. One has only to consider the long preparations of the ancient mystery schools to see this soul preparation at work. Inspirations find us when we are receptive, and inspirations fire up the human being for taking initiative.

I was fascinated to find the following excerpt of a lecture that Rudolf Steiner gave June 26, 1906. He describes common obstacles and four basic laws that accompany them.

10. Ibid., p. 37.

From Rudolf Steiner, June 26, 1906

Students of spiritual science must acquaint themselves with the intimate way that leads to the spiritual world, and they should, above all, learn about obstacles on the path. There are four basic laws that such students must know and live by in order to enter the spiritual world.

First Basic Law:

Whatever you have expressed in words, you have lost all power over in the depth of your soul. Therefore, the best way to lose power is by talking a great deal. There is nothing better than making it a habit to be silent much of the time. Chatter and so on causes demons to carry on lewdness on the astral plane. Today, the spoken word has become a means of destroying human progress. Just recognize the powers of destruction created by reading the countless articles written by modern writers, and realize that all this is read only with the aim of satisfying personal curiosity. Today, the greatest progress would be achieved by printing and reading less.

Second Basic Law:

You destroy your will through whatever you have accumulated in the way of power. From a spiritual point of view, those who have the most power in the outer world will experience the greatest paralysis in their inner will. It is for this reason that esotericists prefer to go humbly through this world rather than as kings. Those who have achieved powerlessness would never trade places with someone in charge of a great nation.

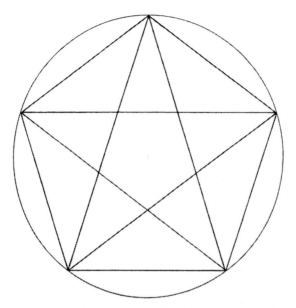

Those who possess great fortunes must care for their wealth and, therefore, are hindered in their will. The more one possesses power, the more one retards the will.

Third Basic Law:

The more you will, the more you lose your inner life of feeling. Whatever we will becomes an obstacle on the spiritual path for our life of feeling. Thus, it will be necessary to develop a disposition toward confining our willing to what the world demands from us and not exercise our will out of inner impulses. In spiritual matters, we advance best if we limit the exercise of our will to what is strictly necessary. Nothing will benefit us more than suppressing our will simply for the sake of suppressing it. In doing so, however, we must learn not to fail in our duties.

Fourth Basic Law:

Too much inner life of feeling destroys thinking. The more easily we are carried away by feelings of great grief or great joy, the more we destroy the purity of our thoughts. To think objectively, we must eliminate the inner life of feeling.

Conclusion:

Students of spiritual science must search and counsel within themselves concerning their foremost task: How can I fulfill the following four admonitions?

Learn to be silent and yours will be power.
Forego the power and yours will be willing.
Forego the willing and yours will be feeling.
Forego the feeling and yours will be knowing.

Lerne Schweigen und dir wird die Macht.
Begib dich der Macht, und dir wird das Wollen.
Begib dich des Wollens und dir wird das Fühlen.
Begib dich des Fuehlens und dir wird Erkenntnis.[11]

What does this fourfold exercise mean for those of initiative? In a world of constant chatter, we need to let go of the word and find silence. This produces inner resources of strength from which we can create. This is only the first step, however. Next, we must let go of the power, the authority, the trappings of any office, in order to free the will. Those who spend most of the day fulfilling the expectations of others will not easily be able to generate new impulses. It is a sad fact that we often give our leaders so many tasks that they become managers, barely coping with daily responsibilities.

11. From a lecture by Rudolf Steiner, Berlin, June 26, 1906.

Along the way, leaders can lose the will to innovate and to initiate new programs, products, and ideas. We need to create leadership roles that have little managerial responsibility and maximum emphasis on vision-building and forward-moving initiatives—less work, more initiative.

Next, we must let go of the will to make room for true, heart-centered feeling instead of passing impressions and emotions. How can we let go of willing? It is not easy, especially for those of us who often have to power our way through the day despite exhaustion. If we can let go, step back, and see situations from a distance, we free an inner space for true experiences of feeling. That feeling, in turn, gives us the possibility of relating and connecting in ways that would never happen when we just power our way through situations. Here, again, we have a reference to the peripheral "I"; the body, or in this case the problem, can become a kind of mirror that can reflect an image and thus help us attain new consciousness.

The final step, as described, is to let go of the feelings to achieve cognition, or knowing. We all know what it is like to be immersed in feelings, swimming as it were in deep waters. There is often a point of emotional blockage, when we cannot see through things clearly. Thus, we again need to practice letting go—this time of our feelings. This can come with reflection (as my wife would say, more blue and less red) when we begin to look at the horizon of phenomena. The distancing generates a perspective that lifts us out of the feeling realm and helps us eventually form reflective thoughts.

Each step of this fourfold journey requires a kind of stepping back and letting go of our usual way of working. Rather than working from the self as embedded in the body and world phenomena, we have to let go and work from the periphery. This frees the human soul for new capacities—in this case new strength, new willing, new feeling, and new knowing. This is a path of freedom that can result in freed capacities for initiative.

Initiative is, in fact, released capacity. What had been held within is now available to the world; a seed is now manifesting in a new form. Instead of wandering along in an evolutionary way, we see involution as a basis for initiative and innovation.

The great challenge for many today is to find the resources through which to act. Rudolf Steiner ends his lecture on the exercises with the image of a pentagram and the following words: "If this pentagram is used, it will be a key to the spiritual world."

> If you can develop a feeling for the relative strength of these impressions and hold them together into *one*, then the harmony of strength is brought about that exists between the forces of the "I" (circle), astral body (outer pentagon), ether body (pentagram), and physical body (inner pentagon).[12]

Isn't it fascinating that the "I" is portrayed as the circle, not the center? This image of the pentagram is thus a true picture of the fourfold human being; the unity of expression is the basis for creative work in the world.

Let us take another step in regard to initiative by going further into the mysterious aspect of the soul we can call the will, for initiative is to willing as consciousness is to freedom. Rudolf Steiner said:

---

12. Steiner, *Wonders of the World,* p. 59 (trans. revised).

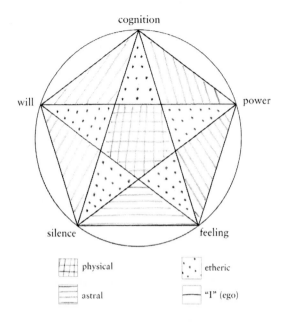

cognition

will

power

silence

feeling

| physical | etheric |
| astral | "I" (ego) |

Before the will can act through human beings here in the physical world, we need the physical body. In the higher worlds, activity of the will is quite different from what it is in the physical world. Thus, as microcosms, we have in us, above all, the forces of soul that bring about our will impulses needed to make good the claim that the "I" is the central governing power of the human soul. Without the will, human beings would never attain "I" consciousness.[13]

This is fascinating. Not only do we need our physical body to act, but the will impulses are also needed for "I" consciousness. We will, and we become. We take initiative, and we realize our humanity. In other words, individuals are able to incarnate completely through the exercise of

13. Ibid., p. 54 (trans. revised).

soul powers such as the will. We can say that the "I," as an expression of the will, occurs when we are most individual, whereas in thinking we can be quite universal. My thoughts can connect with the thoughts of others; we can find a common basis through our thinking, but in willing, we are most unique. We are individuals through our willing.

Initiative is also highly redemptive. What is raw, hard, and jagged in pure will can be taken up by the human being and through initiative made whole. If we sit down to a meal and the table is short one place setting, any one of us can jump up and bring another chair, make a place for another guest. When this happens, everyone is lighter, everyone benefits. The seed of much goodness and love is in initiative; our God-given will to make this Earth a better place.

To help us along the path, the pentagram can become a meditation, for it is indeed an ancient occult sign. If we look at the proportional relationships of the four areas colored below, one can see how the three sheaths of the human being (physical, etheric, astral) are related to the "I," which again is represented as the circle surrounding the whole. Within us, we have the forces of the astral in the yellow, the forces of the etheric in green, and the physical in red.

Certain ratios express the relationship between the size of the geometric shapes in the one aspect to those in another. One can say, for example, as the size of the central pentagon (a) is to the size of the sum of the five triangles (b), so are the forces of the human physical body to the forces of the human etheric body."[14] This meditation, if practiced,

---

14. Ibid., p. 59 (trans. revised).

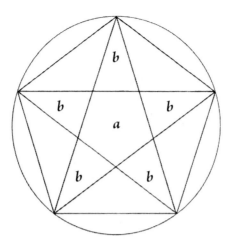

builds inner harmony that can become a resource for wise human initiative.

If freedom and initiative have been the two paths of inquiry thus far, where do they meet? Where do the highest moral forces of free, intuitive human beings meet initiative that aims for the good? We find the convergence in what Rudolf Steiner called "ethical individualism."

People vary in their capacity for intuition. For one person, ideas just bubble up, while another achieves them by much labor. The situations in which people live, and which serve as the scene of their activity, are no less varied. How I act will therefore depend on how my capacity for intuition works in relation to a particular situation. The sum of ideas active within us, the real content of our intuitions, constitutes what is individual in each of us, notwithstanding the universality of the world of ideas. To the extent that the intuitive content turns into action, it is the ethical content of the individual. Allowing this intuitive content to live itself out fully is the highest driving force of morality. At the same time, it is the highest motive of those who realize that, in the end, all other moral principles unite within it. We can call this standpoint *ethical individualism*.[15]

One could say that freedom of action is possible only from the standpoint of ethical individualism. Those who act out of the free substance of intuition (as described) are people of initiative, or ethical individuals. Our world needs such people before we can proceed spiritually to the next chapter of the twenty-first century.

Now let me introduce my new friend, someone who is not actually known by her name but became famous through her actions—the Peace Pilgrim.

If you traveled by car anywhere in North America between 1953 and 1981, you may have seen a silver-haired woman who was cheerfully heeding her calling. She was walking along highways and byways, lingering in small villages and sprawling cities, and talking with people wherever she went. She never disclosed her name, but always referred to herself by the name on her tunic, "Peace Pilgrim." Her cause and her message were simple: *peace.* She said that, once enough of us find inner peace, our institutions will become more peaceful. For twenty-eight years, until her death in 1981, she walked through all fifty states of the U.S. and the ten provinces of Canada, crossing the continent seven times. She stopped to speak for world peace at schools, universities, town meetings, and on TV and radio. It was not just her words that had such a remarkable effect on people, however; it was her being and her way of life.

15. Steiner, *Intuitive Thinking as a Spiritual Path,* pp. 149–150.

When she embarked on her pilgrimage, she gave up all her worldly possessions except the clothes she wore, which included navy-blue slacks and a long-sleeved shirt topped with a lettered tunic. Along the edges of the tunic, front and rear, were pockets that contained all her earthly possessions: a comb, folding toothbrush, pen, map, and her mail. On her feet were simple sneakers, which she replaced every 1,500 miles or so.

> Beneath my outer garments I wear a pair of running shorts and a short-sleeved shirt—so I'm always prepared for an invigorating swim if I pass a river or lake.
>
> As I put on my simple clothing one day after a swim in a clear mountain lake I thought of those who have closets full of clothes to take care of, and who carry heavy luggage with them when they travel. I wondered how people would want to so burden themselves, and I felt wonderfully free. This is me and all my possessions. Think of how free I am! If I want to travel, I just stand up and walk away.[16]

On reading her account more closely, one discovers more than a simple pilgrim who renounced all worldly possessions, who walked until she was given shelter at night (and sometimes had to sleep under the stars), and who fasted until she was offered food, all while walking for twenty-eight years. Under the outer story resides a spiritual story. She describes stages of preparation for her pilgrimage, including finding a "right attitude toward life," bringing one's life into harmony with the

16. *Peace Pilgrim,* pp. 55–56.

universe, simplifying life, and so on.

She speaks, too, of purifying the body (becoming a vegetarian) and purifying thought. "If you realized how powerful your thoughts are, you would never think a negative thought." [17] She mentions the purification of one's motives and acting only for pure service with no thought of personal gain.

Finally, she describes with great clarity certain relinquishments that are necessary for the journey—relinquishing attachments, negative feelings, self-will, and feelings of separation. "Forego the willing and yours will be feeling/Forego the feeling and your will be cognition." [18]

The Peace Pilgrim began her journey, accepting no money and no organizational sponsorship. Everywhere she went, she spoke this simple message:

> *This is the way of peace—overcome evil with good, and falsehood with truth, and hatred with love.* [19]

She was tested along the way. She was arrested for vagrancy; her cell mates remarked that she was the first

17. Ibid., p. 15.
18. From a lecture by Rudolf Steiner, Berlin, June 26, 1906.
19. *Peace Pilgrim*, p. 26.

person ever to come into the communal cell with a smile on her face. She almost died in a snowstorm, at times went for days without food, and had to sleep in the most unusual places. At times, she walked through the night just to stay warm. Along the way, she had a remarkable effect on people, including a violent young man, a bedridden woman, two people who wanted to walk with her, and various fearful people. She prayed a lot at first; then, after some years, her walking *became* a prayer, and she prayed without ceasing.

If you live your life as a prayer, you intensify the prayer beyond all measure....

When you look at things emotionally, you will not see them clearly; when you perceive things spiritually, you will understand....

Ultimate peace begins within...purify your body by sensible living habits, purify your mind by expelling all negative thoughts, purify your motives by casting out any ideas of greed or self-striving and by seeking to serve your fellow human beings, purify your desires by eliminating all wishes for material possessions or self-glorification...and inspire others to do likewise....

One of the ways of working for world peace is to work for more inner peace, because world peace will never be stable until enough of us find inner peace to stabilize it...one little person, giving all of her time to peace, makes news. Many people, giving some of their time, can make history....

Death is a beautiful liberation into a freer life. The limiting clay garment, the body, is put aside.... Could we but see a bit deeper into life, we would grieve at birth and rejoice at death. If we but knew how short is the earth life in comparison with the whole, we would be less troubled with the difficulties of the earth life than we are troubled now with the difficulties of one of our days....

Every good thing you do, every good thing you say, every good thought you think, vibrates on and on and never ceases. The evil remains only until it is overcome by the good, but the good remains forever....

Peace...be still...and know...that I am God.
Peace...be still...and know...that I am.
Peace...be still...and know.
Peace...be still.
Peace...be.
Peace...
Peace...
Peace.[20]

---

20. Ibid., pp. 71–99.

INNOVATION

If we look back in history to some of the most significant changes made over time—the invention of the printing press, the light bulb, penicillin, or the iPhone—it has always been individuals, at times remarkable individuals, who incarnated those new ideas. In education, medicine, farming, and the arts, Rudolf Steiner was an outstanding example of innovation. He was not content to simply perpetuate past practices; through his efforts as an ethical individual, he brought about change in many areas of life. He did not merely repeat what Goethe had started, but took it to the next level. A practical manifestation of ethical individualism is what today is called *innovation*.

As we move farther into the twenty-first century, what can we do as individuals to practice innovation? See the changing dynamics in the world around us not just as threats but as opportunities. True entrepreneurs see "change as an opportunity.[1]"

Innovation can be seen as a diagnostic discipline. It perceives opportunity and responds assertively. Rather than focusing only on major changes such as the Wright brothers' airplane, it is far more helpful to work at perceiving subtle changes in the world and meeting them with initiative. These might include changes in demographics, finances, human values, or expectations. Work involving "cultural creatives" may be of value here.

1.   Drucker, *Innovation and Entrepreneurship*, p. 19.

Peter Drucker says that every three years we should look at our every program, department, and function and ask: Would we start this activity, program, function today? If the answer is "no," then we must be willing to discontinue those activities to make way for new initiatives.

One of the greatest obstacles to initiative is the sheer weight of all that we are already doing. If we are too busy, it is hard to take initiative. Drucker suggests that innovators should be separated from managers. Those who handle the day-to-day work of an organization have a vested interest in perpetuating the status quo. Innovators (and researchers) need to be given space, time, and resources with which to do their work free of institutional responsibilities. Rather than just dealing with "problems" in meetings, we need to see new challenges as opportunities to awaken to new possibilities. What is this situation telling us? What can we do to respond in a new way?

In a world that is volatile, uncertain, complex, and ambiguous, the future will belong to those ethical individuals who, acting out of inner freedom, are able to take the initiative to bring about change.

Whole Systems and Innovation

In today's quickly changing world, old, mechanistic approaches to problem-solving no longer work. As Donella Meadows puts it in her book *Thinking in Systems:*

> Ever since the Industrial Revolution, Western society has benefited from science, logic, and reductionism over intuition and holism. Psychologically and politically we would much rather assume that the cause

of a problem is "out there" rather than "in here." It is almost irresistible to blame something or someone else, to shift responsibility away from ourselves, and look for the control knob, the product, the pill, the technical fix that will make the problem go away.

Serious problems have been solved by focusing on external agents—preventing smallpox, increasing food production, moving large weights and people over long distances. Because they are embedded in larger systems, however, some of our "solutions" have created further problems. And some problems, those most rooted in the internal structure of complex systems, the real messes, have refused to go away.

Hunger, poverty, environmental degradation, economic instability, unemployment, chronic disease, drug addiction and war, persist in spite of the analytical ability and technical brilliance that have been directed toward eradicating them.... That is because they are intrinsically systems problems.... They will yield only when we reclaim our intuition, stop casting blame, see the system as the source of its own problems...we must see things and think about things in a different way."[2]

Donella Meadows, Margaret Wheatley, and others have eloquently described the absolute necessity of expanding our way of seeing to include whole systems. I would like to maintain that this approach, when taken to its ultimate conclusion, must include the spiritual as well as the sense-perceptible aspect of whole systems. After all, Earth and the cosmos are indeed one entire system.

---

2.   Meadows, *Thinking in Systems*, p. 4.

Rudolf Steiner, the foremost esotericist of the twentieth century, consistently took a whole-systems perspective in describing the results of his research. He was intent on reconnecting what had become separated in human knowledge by reuniting many individual subjects into a universal vision he called the wisdom of the human being. Thus, when one takes up a particular topic, such as innovation, one has an immediate opportunity to look at the ramifications from a wider perspective.

In keeping with whole-systems thinking, Steiner described what happens when we sleep. Most of us have little memory of what happens during sleep. Apart from the occasional dream, sleep is generally seen as "time out," a black hole or white wall. Yet Steiner makes the astonishing observation that, thanks to these periods of sleep, those times of darkness, we are able to say "I," to have consciousness of "I." [3] We owe our consciousness of self not to the many things we do all day when awake, but rather to the periods of sleep during the night. "It is the night that makes us real human beings and not mere automata." In a wonderful confirmation of the notion of a peripheral "I" discussed earlier, Steiner says:

> Truth is, we never bring our real and inmost "I" with us from the spiritual world into the physical and earthly; we leave it in the spiritual world, before we came down into earthly life it was in the spiritual world, and it is there again between our falling asleep and our awakening. It stays there always, and if by day—in the present form of human consciousness—we call ourselves an "I," this word is but an indication

---

3. Steiner, *Man as a Picture of the Living Spirit*, p. 8.

of something which is not here in the physical world at all; it only has its *picture* in this world....

We see ourselves correctly only when we say: our true being is in the spiritual world, and what is here of us on Earth is but a picture—an image of our true being."[4]

The eternal self resides in the spiritual world—it is transcendent. The earthly "I" is merely an image of the greater Self during the transitory period we call life.

The fact that the transcendent "I" works during sleep has tremendous implications for innovation and initiative. To put it briefly, sleep is the key to the *resources* we need for creative human action. Most research labs think of funding and grants as a primary concern related to resources. Yet, when we actually have a certain level of material support, the breakthrough moments, the tipping points in innovation, really depend on the human equation in the process. Am I focused, rested, on-task, and, yes, open to the unexpected? For an affirmative answer to these crucial questions, we need to look beyond the resources normally considered when it comes to innovation and find ways to work with a whole-systems approach.

What really takes place when we lie asleep in bed? Outwardly, not much happens. We continue to function biologically, but our consciousness is not present.[5] In addition to the loss of consciousness during sleep, our sense of self, the "I," is also absent. During waking consciousness, the "I" is connected directly with the flow of blood

4. Ibid., p. 9.
5. In anthroposophic literature, this aspect is called the "astral."

and our sense of movement.[6] Likewise, during the day our breathing is very much connected to the astral. During sleep, therefore, a change takes place; a space is created with the departure of the sense of self (the "I") and the change in our consciousness (breathing).

Many meditative practices work directly with breathing and blood circulation to create receptivity and spiritualize the meditator for an influx of non-physical energy. Meditation is a path that works consciously with some of the same elements that occur more or less unconsciously during sleep.

We continue to breathe and our blood continues to circulate during the night. Yet something new also happens. As the "I" withdraws during sleep, it allows for the influx of spiritual forces; beings of the adjoining hierarchy enter the pulsing flow of blood from which the "I" has departed. The particular hierarchy that does so has been called by Rudolf Steiner the angelic realm of *angels, archangels, archai.* Another way of describing these three is *spiritual life, spiritual fire,* and *spiritual personality.* They help us with cosmic reflection and with developing pictorial consciousness and abilities to interact with others. These suprasensory influences work and live in us during sleep.

Similarly, the breathing organs, which have been forsaken by the astral body (consciousness), are now open to the presence of beings in another hierarchy: *exusiai, dynamis, kyriotetes.* These spiritual powers animate and revitalize our organs during sleep by influencing form and motion and by imparting wisdom.

---

6. See Finser, *Organizational Integrity,* p. 148ff.

In terms of our life (etheric) forces, we are unable to replenish ourselves only during the day; we need assistance at night, in this case from the hierarchy of beings identified as *cherubim, seraphim, and thrones.* In this case, however, they work in us both day and night, providing the creative energy we need to continue living. These spiritual powers do so by giving us new possibilities for love (seraphim), harmony (cherubim), and will for life (thrones).

We also have a physical body that requires various kinds of sustenance. Powers of a different order are required here—namely the beings that have been known for millennia as the *Trinity,* the powers of the *Father, Son,* and *Holy Spirit.* Thus, far from being just a collection of atoms and DNA, the human form is a Temple of the Godhead.[7]

To summarize, during sleep constant activity takes place within the human being that does not come only from the physical body itself. In sleep we can gather strength and insight that comes from higher worlds. We are indeed the dwelling place of spiritual beings.

What is the source of our best ideas? We can try to flatter ourselves by believing that ideas are the result of our clever minds. We may also attribute our best achievements to the education of our cultivated minds. Yet if that were true, why are some of the most creative, inventive individuals relatively uneducated—not even what we would call "street smart"?

This cannot be proven, of course, but I would like to affirm my conviction that there are spiritual archetypes (connected to the hierarchies mentioned) that can work *through human beings when they have prepared the*

---

7.   Steiner, "Man as a Picture of the Living Spirit," p. 11.

ground. Part of such preparation involves living mindfully, preparing the body as a vessel for inspiration, and appropriate sleep practices. This relates to how we prepare—how we enter and exit sleep to access the natural spiritual resources available to us.

We all know that creative problem solving and working through the challenges that each day brings is enormously affected by the quality of sleep we have had the night before. We are able to do so much more when we have slept well (which does not always equate with the number of hours of sleep). But if we can do a review of the day before falling asleep, if we can attend to the inner content of our thoughts during the day, we can influence significantly the quality of sleep. Waking gradually and recalling any dreams, or even just the quality of the sleep journey, can also help. Some people keep a sleep journal.

Creative problem solving, indeed innovation itself, can thus be seen as the concrete expression of spiritual archetypes that are merely waiting to be realized. There is a solution to every problem, every challenge, but we as humans must become much more adept at removing hindrances to the in-streaming of these solutions!

According to Donella Meadows, "The ability to self-organize is the strongest form of system resilience. A system can evolve and survive almost any change by changing itself."[8] She goes on to say that self-organization is based on a highly variable stock of information and that this variety is intimately connected to human creativity. Just as economists (and others) worship technology as a solution to all of our problems, and just as biologists see

---

biodiversity as fundamental to our survival on Earth, innovators and those who work with human potential must consider whole-system, self-organizing dynamics as the key to productive change. Technology without biodiversity could leave us without a viable planet. Likewise, the very future of those of us who live on this planet depends on our resilience and value-based, self-initiated action that considers the whole system, not just our personal self-interest. The intricate human processes we call innovation go to the very heart of our human condition. Innovation is not a luxury; it is a necessity.

In Praise of Solitude

In an address given at West Point in October 2009, William Deresiewicz urged the plebes to practice introspection, concentration, and nonconformity. With considerable urgency, he described the present-day challenge:

> We have a crisis of leadership in America because our overwhelming power and wealth, earned under earlier generations of leaders, made us complacent, and for too long we have been training leaders who only know how to keep the routine going. Who can answer questions but don't know how to ask them. Who can fulfill goals, but don't know how to set them. Who think about how to get things done, but not whether they're worth doing in the first place. What we have now are the greatest technocrats the world has ever seen, people who have been trained to be incredibly good at one specific thing, but who have no interest in anything beyond their area of expertise. What we don't have are people who can

think for themselves; people who can formulate a new way of doing things, a new way of looking at things; people with vision.[9]

Deresiewicz went on to cite a Stanford study on multi-tasking. They found that the more people multi-task, the worse they become at other mental abilities, including multi-tasking itself:

> [Researchers] found that in every case the high multi-taskers scored worse. They were worse at distinguishing between relevant and irrelevant information and ignoring the latter. They were more easily distracted. They were more unorganized, unable to keep information in the right conceptual boxes and retrieve it quickly. And they were even worse at the very thing that defines multi-tasking: switching between tasks. Multi-tasking, in short, impairs your thinking. Thinking is not about learning other people's ideas or memorizing a body of information. It requires concentrating on one thing long enough to develop an idea of your own.[10]

No wonder it is so hard to find innovators today. We are multi-tasking our way out of even having time for original thoughts. William Deresiewicz makes a plea for reading books and the training in thinking that comes with following another person's narrative. In fact, many of the greatest works in literature took a long time to write (that is, much thinking preceded writing). T. S. Eliot wrote about 150 pages of poetry over a twenty-five-year career, which works out to about a half a page per month.

9.   Deresiewicz, "Solitude and Leadership," p. 48–53.
10.   Ibid., p. 51.

In contrast to constant immersion in Facebook and Twitter, which bombard people with a deluge of other people's thoughts, Emerson said that "he who should inspire and lead his race must be defended from traveling with the souls of other men, from living, breathing, reading, and writing in the daily, timeworn yoke of their opinions."[11]

To think, to develop real ideas that have staying power, one needs introspection, and introspection is done best in solitude or in a long conversation with a good friend. There is even such a thing as inner conversations with oneself. Most of my writing occurs first in this kind of inner dialogue before it finds a footprint on the page. Ideas have a way of circulating back, moving in and out of connectedness with other ideas, and suddenly there is something new, perhaps even an inspiration.

Perhaps more than at any time in history, we need to carve out a quiet space consciously for real thinking, which is strenuous inner work when done right. Solitude can provide space for reflection that can mature into new ideas. Creative thinking is bound up with inspiration and innovation. These capacities are essential for the kind of leadership our world needs today.

Anthroposophy in the Twenty-first Century

For those of us working out of Anthroposophy in the years ahead, we need to be mindful of remaining hindrances to innovation and free thinking—two more of the ghosts of the past referred to earlier.

---

11. Emerson, *Essays*, pp. 44–45.

First, the intellectual soul has helped us attain greater freedom over the past centuries. Humanity has started to ask the right questions. Yet the Greco-Roman way of thinking has crept too often into our conceptualization of Anthroposophy. The work of the Anthroposophical Society has been burdened by some individuals who have ingested anthroposophic concepts and rattled them around in abstract constructs like so much loose change in one's pockets. Rather than theorizing Anthroposophy, we need to *practice* Anthroposophy, a method that can be applied to all life situations if we only develop the capacities to do so. If the intellectual soul has helped us ask questions, it will be the consciousness soul that provides real answers.

> The more the epoch of the consciousness soul develops and the more it emerges out of the intellectual residues of its immediate past, the more this soul will be recognized in its true nature. And its true nature is indeed already highly spiritual. But spiritual means sovereign, creative and active, inwardly aflame with the fire of love and enthusiasm for the mysteries of the world and of man, and thoroughly irradiated and penetrated with the forces of clear, precise, and living thinking and imagination.[12]

Another hindrance from the past has to do with *theosophy* and the more mystical traditions in spiritual history. Too many people today still treat Anthroposophy as if it were theosophy. Their mystical, at times unthinking, and worshipful absorption of Anthroposophy as a kind of tonic does little to further the development of our Society,

---

12. Ben Aharon, *The New Experience of the Supersensible,* p. 4.

let alone humankind. The more conscious path called for in Anthroposophy can be difficult and even painful at times, but unless we do the research, we will be seen by the world simply as the legacy of Rudolf Steiner. To enter the twenty-first century spiritually, we cannot be sleeping theosophists or Roman orators; rather, we need to be self-aware meditants who are seen in the world as people of initiative. For this we need arduously to cultivate inner substantiality and the capacities described earlier. If we are inwardly alive and working as ethical individuals and agents of change, Anthroposophy can open the heart of humanity.

Summary

- To help us in the years ahead, we need an "initiative society" that counteracts the adversarial powers by supporting the freed I, the individuality of each human being as an eternal being.

- The Anthroposophical Society can become known as supporting initiative—recognizing innovative practices and people even before the rest of the world catches on.

- We can celebrate remarkable human beings such as the Peace Pilgrim, even if they are not "card-carrying" members, as examples of ethical individualism.

- We can stand, inspired by the *Representative of Humanity*, between the polarizing powers of

Lucifer and Ahriman, finding the balance, the way of the Christ.

- We can be more of an NGO, a service organization that supports socially responsible efforts across the globe through endorsements and partnerships.

- And especially through the School for Spiritual Science, we can promote and support original research that becomes an ever greater resource for those seeking answers to the deeper questions of our time, whether they be in science, medicine, agriculture, or education.

Can we hear the cry of humanity today? Can we truly perceive the needs of our fellow human beings? Are we willing to suffer their questions, walk their path, and be there with all our resources when needed?

For the years ahead, we cannot become like the Essenes, living pure lives apart from humanity. We need to take the renewed substance of spiritual science and take initiative in the world. Anthroposophy is not designed as a form of entertainment in spiritual clothing. Rather, it is an invitation to human beings to develop themselves toward freedom and initiative.

Living thinking, Peace Pilgrim-like service, creative initiative means working with the Christ impulse in our twenty-first century. Our work, especially our struggles, can lead to rejuvenating forces for our Earth if we are awake and active. Being awake means conscious freedom, being active spells initiative. Indeed, "every word in Anthroposophy, when it is rightly expressed, is in reality an asking, a reverent plea—a plea that the spirit may descend to human beings."[13] May our words spoken on these matters become an invocation to spirit working on Earth.

---

13. Steiner, *Truth-Wrought-Words and Other Verses*, p. 191.

PLANETARY LEADERSHIP

Preface

In my 2007 book *Organizational Integrity*, I introduced the notion of planetary types, mainly from a self-aware-ness and relational point of view. That brief chapter is reprinted in this chapter. However, in the years since that original piece, I have done further research in regard to the role of planetary influences, particularly concerning leadership applications and biography. These additional considerations are discussed in the second and third chapters of the present book.

The urgent state of our current world situation and the desperate search for better leadership has propelled me forward in this line of inquiry. So many people have what I call "old concepts" of leadership, often associated with hierarchy or position. Because of our checkered history of leadership around the world (dictatorships, broken promises, athletes on steroids, and so on), many people have thrown the baby out with the bathwater. People have become cynical and express their deep disrespect for today's leaders. In doing so, they have sometimes made it excruciatingly difficult for leaders to exercise leadership. One might say that, given the general mood of today, all leaders are suspect. As a result, there is little trust; fewer and fewer people are willing to serve, and our organizations and institutions are caught in a kind of stalemate. Consider the recent history in Washington, D.C., and the political situation surrounding the passage of health-care legislation, or European attempts to find real solutions to dealing with debt problems. It has become increasingly difficult for anyone to exercise real leadership, and almost impossible to collaborate and find meaningful compromise.

The failure of leadership today comes at a tremendous cost, both financially and in terms of human resources. Our inability to act means that many urgent needs are not addressed, including unemployment and economic instability, poverty and hunger, and the environment. Giving speeches and posturing is no substitute for leadership. The problem is that the "old concepts" no longer work.

How Can We Reimagine and Even Reinvent Leadership?

I have long advocated for greater attention to the development of leaders and movement away from dependence on random volunteerism in many of our nonprofits or the democratic process of choosing the lesser of two evils. Yet before people and organizations will be willing to invest more in leadership development, *we need to change our concepts of leadership*. A change in consciousness often precedes outer change, and these reflections on planetary leadership are intended to provoke new questions and debate. Because of this, at the end of this piece I have included lead topics and questions to stimulate conversation and a review of established practices. If we can introduce new concepts into our schools, businesses, governmental agencies, and communities, then we can effect change, even if only gradually.

I. Planetary Influences

The metals that reside in the earth have a connection to their surroundings, not only in terms of geography but also the greater cosmos. The wise teachers of olden times knew of the connections between the metals and the planets, and it is part of our quest for organizational health to reawaken the living relationships that exist between Earth, the planets, and the human body. In this chapter we will consider the Greek gods, their Roman counterparts, and their connections to the metals and aspects of human physiology.

Chronos was a Titan, an elder god, who ruled for untold ages. The Titans had great strength and were of an enormous size. Chronos ruled the Titans until his son Zeus dethroned him and seized power. In her book *Mythology,* Edith Hamilton writes,

> The Romans said that when Jupiter, their name for Zeus, ascended the throne, Saturn [*Chronos*] fled to Italy and brought in the Golden Age, a time of perfect peace and happiness, which lasted as long as he reigned.[1]

In Greek mythology, when the sons of Chronos drew lots for their share of the universe, the sea fell to Poseidon, Hades ruled the underworld, and **Zeus** became the supreme ruler of all, lord of the sky, the rain god, the cloud gatherer, and the one who could wield the awful thunderbolt. Greater than all the other divinities, Zeus was nevertheless fallible and could be duped by Poseidon or his wife Hera.

1.   Hamilton, *Mythology,* p. 24.

Zeus and Hera had a son called Ares (Mars), who became the God of War. Even his parents detested him.

> Homer calls him murderous, bloodstained, the incarnate curse of mortals; and, strangely, a coward, too, who bellows with pain and runs away when he is wounded. [2]

The Romans liked their Mars better than the Greeks liked Ares. Phoebus Apollo, the son of Zeus and Leto, was born on the island of Delos. He delighted the Olympians as he played on his golden lyre; he is featured in poetry and known for having taught human mortals the healing arts. Above all, Apollo is the God of Light "in whom is no darkness at all and so he is the God of Truth." [3]

Some years ago, I had the pleasure of visiting the site of Apollo's oracle at Delphi. Despite the passage of many years, I was able to experience the clarity and vision of the place—the clear air, the sharp outline of stone against blue sky, and the sacred ground that had been the meeting place for people with urgent questions to ask. In ancient times, people from all over the world came to the sacred springs of wisdom for answers to their questions. Seekers for truth listened in rapt attention as the priestess of the oracle went into a trance before speaking. With vapor rising, the words would pour forth, at times incoherently. The word *phoebus* means "brilliant" or "shining." Indeed, for ancient Greece, Apollo was the Sun God.

His twin sister Artemis was the lady of wild things, a hunter, and protector of youth. When a woman died a

---

2. Ibid., p. 34.
3. Ibid., p. 30.

swift and painless death, she, too, was slain by the silver arrows of Artemis. If Apollo was the Sun, Artemis was the Moon. One can picture the lovely hunter flashing through the forest by the silvery light of the moon. The cypress was her sacred tree, and she loved all wild animals, especially the deer.

Aphrodite was celebrated as the Goddess of Love and Beauty. She beguiled both gods and mortals and laughed sweetly, yet would mock those she had conquered. She was the irresistible goddess who stole the wits of even the wise. Some say she sprang from the foam of the sea[4] and that she had a special connection to the islands of Cyprus and Cythera:

> The breath of the west wind bore her
> Over the sounding sea,
> Up from the delicate foam,
> To wave-ringed Cyprus, her isle,
> And the Hours golden-wreathed
> Welcomed her joyously.[5]
>
> —HOMER

Finally we introduce the winged Hermes, messenger of the gods. Graceful and swift of motion, his feet were winged sandals; wings were on his low-crowned hat as well. Most cunning of all the gods, he was also the master thief who began his first day of life by stealing Apollo's herds. When forced to give them back, Hermes made amends with Apollo by presenting him with a lyre that he had just made out of a tortoise's shell. Hermes later became the solemn guide of the dead, the divine herald

---

4. The Greek word *aphros* means "foam."
5. Hamilton, p. 32.

who accompanied souls to their last home. As messenger on all sorts of errands for the gods, Hermes appears more frequently in Greek tales than any other god.

To summarize, we can list the Greek gods with their Roman counterparts:

Chronos	Saturn
Zeus	Jupiter
Ares	Mars
Apollo	Apollo
Aphrodite	Venus
Hermes	Mercury
Artemis	Diana

It is fascinating to note that the Roman designations begin to veer more in the direction of the planets known to this day. If one substitutes *Sun* for *Apollo,* and *Moon* for *Diana,* we have the planets with their corresponding metals:[6]

Saturn	lead
Jupiter	tin
Mars	iron
Sun	gold
Venus	copper
Mercury	mercury
Moon	silver

Working with these connections, Rudolf Steiner showed in his medical lectures how we may consider lead the result of certain "undisturbed effects" of Saturn; tin the "undisturbed effects" of Jupiter; iron that of Mars; and so on.[7] Spirit and matter correspond to each other; there is a

6. Pelikan, *Secrets of Metals,* p. 39.

7. Steiner, *Introducing Anthroposophical Medicine,* p. 94.

spiritual counterpart for everything on Earth.[8] In the old manuscripts of Paracelsus, one of the first physicians, one finds that the word *planet* did not describe only the shining globe we know in the night sky or through our telescope. Rather, he viewed the orbits of the planets as spheres of motion around Earth. Thus, one had a "moon sphere" (the "planet" closest to Earth) and a "Saturn sphere" (farthest from Earth). The planets were not simply "things" but orientation points. In Greek mythology, the spheres of motion were divine beings, or "gods." Today, we can speak of leaders who are echoes of the greater cosmic picture. Instead of planets orbiting the universe or metals trapped in the earth, leaders have organizations in which they try to activate spheres of motion. Wherever there is movement, there is the possibility of creativity and initiative.

Now let us look more closely at what I call the "planetary types" and how they can help us achieve collaborative leadership when taken to a new level of consciousness.

The Saturn Type

Such persons cultivate their inner world with great energy but generally have poor relationships with the outer world. They do not relate to the moment, or the present, but tend to see everything in the context of the past. So when an issue comes up for consideration, the Saturn type tends to say, "Five years ago when we faced this situation..."; or, "The last time we did this, we found that..." Saturn types are so focused on the past that they find it hard to make decisions. They need much time to assimilate events

---

8. "Undisturbed effects" are the direct influences between the planets and metals.

and facts. It is hard for them to spring into action, because they would rather take more time to consider precedents and past examples. Although they appear outwardly inactive, they have many thoughts, even profound ones. I have found that a Saturn type will often wait to speak until the end of a meeting and then say something that not only summarizes, but also goes further than would another hour of discussion. However, Saturn types can be awkward in practical matters (they are typically not good car mechanics), and they tend to be easily offended. Life is generally experienced as a burden. Their virtue is loyalty; their vice is spite. Saturn types can often be overlooked because many of their talents are hidden.

How can we work with Saturn types? We need to take a deep interest in them, prepare inwardly for conversation, and give advance notice of what will happen so that impressions become a memory, their favored way of processing information.[9] Rather than spring a conversation on a Saturn colleague at work, you can say, "Could we get together tomorrow to talk about...?" This helps Saturn types create a memory picture of the introduction, inwardly reference the topic, and come to the meeting prepared.

The Mercury Type

The Mercury type is much more common than the Saturn type. In the life of Mercury types, as Max Stibbe says in his *Seven Soul Types*:

Chaos is generally the rule. They jump from one thing to another, and undertake a million and one different tasks that seem to happen their way by chance. They

9. Stibbe, *The Seven Soul Types*, p.28.

know all kinds of people, make friends with everyone, and are exceedingly adept at dealing with people. [10]

The Mercury type can observe things and people with great acuteness and have the capacity for corrective thought and change of thinking. They always seem to be in motion, dancing through life as it were, but they are inwardly quite passive because they are led by outer impressions. They live in the details and are reactive, both to things around them and to their own feelings. Whatever is happening in the moment is of utmost importance.

The virtue of the Mercury type is their light-footed cleverness; their vice can be a kind of superficiality that can border on dishonesty. Remember the previous reference to Mercury and thieves. If one is in a workplace situation with Mercury types, encourage them to do even more detailed observations and elicit comparisons and reflections so they are stimulated inwardly and bring more thoughtfulness to their actions.

The Mars Type

In many ways this is the direct opposite of the self-conscious type. Here the outer world is paramount, and action is preferred over reflection. Instead of the past, the Mars type looks continually to the future. Action is a means of establishing a relationship with the outside world, and the Mars type feels that it is better to "do something" than nothing at all. These people are goal oriented, they push obstacles aside, and they can be quite rude at times, even forceful. The Romans were known as Mars people, and strong personalities in history belong to this group as

10. Ibid, p. 52.

well, including Napoleon, Voltaire, and Elizabeth I. When attacked from the outside, as was the case for England and the invasion of the Spanish Armada during the reign of Elizabeth I, the Mars type can rise to greatness.

In working with the Mars type, it is important to maintain a certain inner composure in the face of their forceful outbursts. Indeed, their virtue is courage, but their vices are anger, excessive zeal, and the tendency to give free rein to their passions. Much of our modern world caters to the Mars types. "Just send in the military" is a common answer to many of the world's problems. The necessary transformation here calls for more and more people to fight their inner battles within instead of externalizing them. This can mean taking a walk to overcome feelings of anger before letting it out in a meeting. If Mars types can learn from their inner conflicts, they can then bring the resulting wisdom to future efforts.

The Moon Type

Moon types are wonderful mirrors of their environment. This is possible because they are inwardly passive and have few defenses against the outside world. You can notice this reflective quality even in their language, as they quickly begin to use the words and expressions of those around them. They are artistically inclined and can absorb large amounts of intellectual content while not necessarily doing any original thinking. Moon types often have a poetic inclination, yet they can give in to unconscious instincts.

Historical examples of Moon types from the eighteenth century include Louis XV and Louis XVI of France, both of whom were considered indecisive and unable to reform the monarchy. They illustrate this point by Max Stibbe: "The passive element in the soul of this type can give rise to excesses which are best counteracted by artistic creativity." [11] Indeed, the virtue of the Moon type is an artistic inclination and circumspection, while their vice is passivity, even licentiousness.

When you are in the workplace with Moon types, try to get behind their mirrors and the images they portray by asking probing questions and requesting amplification. As with all the other types, it is important to build on their virtues. Artistic work is an ideal way for Moon types to stimulate a connection with the outer world and to promote activity that goes beyond imaging. The arts help us observe more accurately, something the Moon types need to develop.

The Venus Type

These folks are often closely related to the Moon types and are often female. The Venus types have an intimate, though passive, relationship to the outer world. They react to everything out of sympathy or antipathy, liking or disliking, or at least responding with personal opinion. They form judgments of all that happens around them. Thus the vice of the Venus type can be a kind of one-sidedness that restricts things to the life of feeling. The extreme can be greed. Their virtue is a disposition that always seeks to have an object or person for their love and affection.

In the workplace it is helpful to encourage Venus types to modify and amend their initial instinctive judgments.

---

11. Ibid., p. 37.

Rather than just let them respond out of love or dislike for people or proposals, try and get them to get engaged, to do work that brings a broader perspective. Activity in the will and in thinking can balance the preference for feeling responses. An example would be to ask: Have you read any books recently that illustrate this situation? This promotes reflection that is lifted to a more objective plane.

The Jupiter Type

This type is not so common (to the relief of many), because this regal soul can create all sorts of problems in the workplace if allowed to rule unchecked. They are so intent on achieving a balance between the inner and outer world that any hint of chaos is seen as an abomination. The Jupiter type tries at all costs to create order. These folks can assess all problems in an instant and want to solve them right away. Their goal is to end up with complete, all-encompassing solutions and grand designs. They act with calm assurance and are willing to go all the way in grand style. Remember our reference to Zeus. The poet Goethe with his far-reaching abilities as poet, writer, scientist, and artist, was a Jupiter type.

The virtue of these folks is that they have great capacity for hope; they always strive for the big picture. "While we are at it, let's build the gym, too." Their vice can be arrogance and a feeling that those who do not live on Olympus are inferior. In the workplace, it is important to meet the Jupiter types by having entertained their ideas oneself and considered their images of greatness. Try to see their widely ranging concepts and the perspective from the top of the mountain. This helps one gain entry to their shining castles.

The Sun Type

Just as gold can be placed at the center of all metals, it is possible to strive toward a state of harmonious integration of all the planetary types. We can take all the positive attributes of the other types and reach an dynamic balance between the inner and the outer and the reactive and the proactive, as well as among the activities of willing, feeling, and thinking. This type, the Sun folks, work from the heart. They are seen as kind and considerate, and their goodness endears them to others. This final stage, the Sun type, can be achieved by individuals or can arise from intense collaboration of the many "planets" working together in our organizations.

During youth, human beings are influenced most by Saturn, Jupiter, and Mars (whose orbits are outside Earth's orbit). In later life, people are influenced more by the inner planets (with orbits between that of Earth and the Sun), Venus, Mercury, and the Moon. Now we can ask: Is there such a thing as youth and old age in organizations? One might assign observational tasks based on the planets and metals. For example, if we have a clear picture of the quality of Mars and its earthly counterpart of iron, can we see a preponderance of energy, strength, youthful enthusiasm, and courage in the organization?

It is important to keep the mind open to the possibilities of these types and suspend previous assumptions that can interfere with clear perceptions of those around us in the workplace. It is part of human nature to draw conclusions based on a sliver of information, which clouds our perception. In my consulting work, for instance, I often receive an initial inquiry on the phone that "presents" a need or request. I have learned to be especially careful not to take the "presenting issue or question" at face value. Rather, I see it as an invitation to explore further and involve more people in my first site visit. The "planet" of the person calling me should not be allowed to prevail as the "signature" of the whole organization.

In addition to the individual planetary qualities, when looking at leadership traits in an organization it is sometimes helpful to consider typical "pairs" that occur in teams. A tendency exists to match the more active type of one planetary leader with the passive qualities of another. For example, Saturn is often paired with Venus (in relationships, too), Jupiter with Mercury, and Mars with Moon. It is natural to have one leader oriented more toward internal matters (for example, Steve Ballmer, CEO of Microsoft), and one geared more toward the public (Bill Gates, for example, the founder of Microsoft, who seems to enjoy introducing products and meeting the public). This planetary pairing can help maximize each person's potential while serving to balance the competing needs of the organization. It sometimes happens instinctively or spontaneously, but I am suggesting a more deliberate approach based on the increased understanding of human beings that can come with planetary types and other considerations in this book.

So what does a healthy organization look like? We are used to describing dysfunction, with the result that less attention has been placed on organizational health. Just as we need heart, lung, and liver to function properly for our physical health, to achieve organizational health we need to see the correspondences between human beings and larger influences. I would like to draw these connections, this time among the metals described earlier, the planets, and the human organs:

SATURN	lead	spleen
JUPITER	tin	liver
MARS	iron	gall
SUN	gold	heart
VENUS	copper	kidneys
MERCURY	mercury	lungs
MOON	silver	reproductive organs and glands

Medicine must not act without the participation of heaven; it must act together with it. Therefore, you must separate the medicine from the earth so it will obey the will of the stars and be guided by them. (Paracelsus)

As we consider the marvelous completeness of the starry heavens, let us contemplate several questions. Can we imagine an organizational structure in which all the planets revolve in harmony? Can our leadership needs be met by different metals at different times, depending on the immediate tasks? Can we use the language of the heart, lung, kidneys, and other organs to speak of whole-systems work that promotes health and regeneration?

Having looked at several aspects of leadership, the next chapter will return to the theme of group dynamics and reveal ways that leaders can use group geometry to achieve greater success.

2: Applications

One of the challenges of transforming consciousness is our tendency toward abstractions—that is, taking in ideas, old or new, and simply holding them with only our intellect. When ideas remain abstract, they become like the stones in the proverbial stomach of the wolf; they rattle around but may not affect the world around us.

The tendency toward abstraction is a huge challenge for humanity today. For instance, in the world of finance, mortgages and loans used to be based on a relationship with a local banker. Today, they are a matter of large governmental agencies and complex financial instruments. The recent subprime debacle was caused in part through the use of abstract financial tools that very few understood well and had little basis in reality, such as one's ability to pay. Whether in health care or outcome-based teaching in schools, we are surrounded everywhere by abstractions that often leave us inwardly cold and unchanged.

Thus, it is of great importance to me to take the notions of planetary types described in this book and give some consideration to practical examples and applications. Although there are limitations to these considerations, the reader will at least be encouraged to reflect similarly and try to find ways to use these leadership styles in everyday life. *Real ideas thus become ideals that change awareness and lead to renewed activity.*

The Moon Type

As a mirror of light, the moon type reflects ideas and impressions from the environment. Deep inside, Moon types may harbor profound secrets and even wisdom from past experiences, but this often remains hidden as they interact as reflectors of the outer world. The mystery of this type of person is the dual nature of inner seclusion and the outer play of interaction. Indeed, a public person can often be a very private person, as well.

Good examples of this type are members of the House of Representatives, as well as many other public officials. Having been to a variety of political events over the years, I am frequently astonished at how good such individuals are at absorbing the popular will surrounding them and then reflecting those ideas back in their speeches. New Hampshire has the honor of being the first primary state, and many residents there get to meet the many presidential hopefuls in small-town settings. I have marveled at the ability of such politicians to pick up the views of those asking questions and then reflect them back as part of their answers. When it works, the people feel validated and heard, while the politician scores points with the audience. Being responsive is part of the art of politics.

Thus, we see that there is value to representing the views of others. Democracy at its best allows ordinary citizens not only a vote every few years, but also the hope that someone in government will reflect their views when making decisions. Thus, "government by the people and for the people."

What is the meaning of "representation"? When I have been in this role, I try to carry an inner picture of the person or group I am representing. I try to think like those I represent, because it is impossible to know in every instance what our constituents would want us to do. Consequently, one has to become like them, absorb and carry their ideas.

A true representative often juggles diverse needs and wishes and even creates a mosaic of those views in speeches and in actions.

The danger of the Moon type is that the inner sanctum—one's foundation of values and beliefs—may be neglected or forgotten. One can become like a crater on the moon, hardened and inwardly cold. A representative can become a product of his or her surroundings, losing one's inner foundation, the inner flame. This is one of the reasons that so many politicians "go bad" after too many years in office. One's inner compass, once lost, is hard to regain.

In schools, it is often a challenge when a parent is asked to "represent" the body of parents as a member of the PTA or school board. Such parents usually try their best, but when it comes down to the ebb and flow of discussion in meetings people can really represent only themselves. Votes are taken and decisions made that become part of a larger process. Afterward, however, the constituency (the other parents) may complain that their "representative" did not truly represent "our views." Many such representatives often end up quitting, feeling frustrated and underappreciated.

Can we really represent the ideas of others? If we possess great integrity and inner discipline, it is possible to carry an idea that originated with someone else. We have to make it our own in the process. However, there are serious limitations when representing an entire group, whether a parent body, faculty, or town. We can carry some of the wishes of a larger group, but eventually we have to act as individuals.

I have concluded that we cannot remain only representatives and the reflecting Moon. If you are on a board, you are not just a representative, but also a board member, with all the rights and responsibilities that go with that office. One can enter a meeting for a few minutes and give a report, but with the right to vote one has to take a stand on the issues, just as any other member must. Group process calls for decisions based on the collective insight of those present, not just a tally of votes that represent different perspectives. Such a misunderstanding is one of the reasons that some sessions of Congress fail to accomplish much. If everyone is merely representing, no one moves beyond fixed views, and stalemates become the norm. Such are the limitations of Moon-type leadership.

Key words for Moon-style leadership:
responsive, representative, reproduction,
mirror image

The Saturn Type

In many ways, the Saturn style of leadership is the opposite of the Moon style. Instead of reflecting back what is received, the Saturn type tends to absorb and store vast amounts of information, perhaps for later use. Thus, the Saturn type can appear self-absorbed. When the Saturn type does share, it is through stories, historical context, and gradual revelation of what has been stored up in the past.

Scholars and specialists are the ideal professional applications of this style of working. We can imagine a person spending years researching some obscure aspect of science or history, planning "someday" to publish the results. However, that day is often postponed, like the never-finished dissertation, as more and more information is gathered. These folks go for depth and synthesis and are often seen as pack rats. They are attracted to traditional academia and can seem distant and even aloof. They are not fully present, but seem to work with internal processes that may have little to do with the conversation at hand.

These types are reluctant to become formal leaders; dealing with the here-and-now is seen as a compromise, though they are occasionally willing to sit on committees and provide valuable expertise. In larger group discussions, they often withhold their insights until the end of the meeting, and even then need to be drawn out. Nonetheless, their expertise can be valuable, often leading people to say, "If only we had known this before, we could have saved ourselves a lot of time." Saturn types orbit way out there, and we need to reach out to them.

In working with Saturn types, I have found that we can break down their reticence if we are dealing with an issue they see as vital to institutional integrity or survival. If we can frame issues in a larger context, Saturn types may step forward despite themselves and provide a kind of quiet guidance. Saturn types are often individuals of amazing knowledge and expertise, even wisdom, and we need their participation.

In groups, we need the Saturn influence to balance the influence of Mars and Mercury types, who simply want to move forward, sometimes blindly. Saturn leaders will make sure we see the various perspectives and learn from experience. They thus tend to slow the pace, and colleagues can become frustrated at behavior that seems obstructionist.[12] Saturn types can also become a kind of conscience for the group, reminding everyone of past agreements, successes, and failures. We need to be mindful of the past in making decisions for the future.

I have found that facilitation plays an extraordinarily important role in managing all leadership styles. In reference to the Saturn type, however, the relationship to the facilitator is crucial. Saturn types must trust the facilitator; otherwise, they clam up. It helps when the facilitator can have a few words with the Saturn type before a meeting—preferably a day or two earlier—so that the Saturn type can form memories of the topic to hold during the group's conversation. Memories become more to Saturn types than simply a security blanket; they become a path to the present and a way into the discussion. A good facilitator will draw the Saturn type into the open with a question such as, "What happened last time we planned this event?" The wisdom of the Saturn type will then start to flow into the group, with the result that some sage advice might be shared.

As we will see, Saturn is the planetary type of maturity—ages fifty-six to sixty-three in terms of human biography. We have to be especially careful when selecting leaders for established organizations, making certain that there are not too many Saturn types within leadership groups. If the organization or business is naturally in a Saturn mode itself, having too many leaders

12. Watch for Saturn types sitting on the periphery of a meeting, just as the actual planet orbits at a great distance from the center.

of that type can make everything seem like a documentary. Sharing and conversing may be rich in content, but it may cause the organization to have difficulty moving forward. Clients who come from different planetary impulses may drift away and cease to engage. A parent once said to me, "If I hear that story about the founding of the school one more time I will puke." Just as we value diversity as a cultural value, we also need to look at organizations as an invitation to all types of people, not just those who value the stories of the past.

Key words for the Saturn type: memories, distance, depth, specialization, historian of the universe

The Jupiter Type

Active, creative problem solvers, Jupiter types love large challenges. Like architects, these folks can visualize many possible solutions and love applying creative thinking to solve the weighty problems at hand. Their thinking can be both flexible and vigorous. A solution can assume a grand scale when allowed to run unchecked. A simple building addition may become an atrium or even an auditorium. Nothing is impossible.

Thoughts live in forms, as known to the ancient Greek philosopher Plato. These forms are realities. Our thoughts exist in the world as creative powers and are just as real, even more so the chairs, tables, and "things" we usually occupy. Jupiter types have an instinctive feel for the creative potential of active thinking and for the formative power of thoughts. They can imagine solutions and love to bring the thought forms into visible reality.

Whereas Saturn types love to tell us about the past, Jupiter types are strongly connected to the present. They live in the here-and-now. Thus, if there is a problem to be solved, rather than sending it out to a committee or undertaking a study, Jupiter types will want to engage immediately. Why postpone what we can do today?

These great designers and creative problem solvers have to work with the lifelong challenge not to over-commit; rather, they must take on what is truly doable. If we over-reach, even the most creative plans can eventually crumble. Thus, every action, even our thoughts, needs to be focused on what is essential in a task; other aspects need to be set aside. For this, the other types can help channel the energy of Jupiter types in a way that leads to achievable outcomes.

In working with groups, I have found that it is important to engage the energy and vision of Jupiter types early in the process. They need a large playing field to feel at home. They are great at working with an amorphous, multifaceted situation and feel frustrated if too many boundary lines are drawn early in the process. For example, they respond well to the questions: What do we need? How can we make this work? What are the possible solutions? They respond less well if one stipulates from the start a certain budget, team membership, or limitations in time or effort. Jupiter types can help us see new possibilities, and for that, they need some space in which to be creative.

Once the project has been worked out, Jupiter types are perfectly willing to lend their time and energy to carry it out, but they need to feel that time was given for the creative, picture-forming process at the start.

This brings me to an interesting observation about group work. Often, we are limited not by the scarcity of financial resources that we all complain about, but by the ways we work with the leadership styles as a group. We tend to think that money is the all-determining factor in many matters these days, but money is in fact only the outer manifestation of the focused energy and capacities of the leaders. Why do some organizations and businesses grow while others shrink? The ebb and flow of an organism is caused more by the ways people interact than by the resources already manifest. One might say that capital is the result of past spiritual activity; in using money, we are living off past achievements. What is so desperately needed is a greater awareness of how to build future capital.

Most of the resources available today actually remain invisible and have yet to be realized. Unlocking these resources is the great mystery of our time. Just as the earth contains mineral deposits of gold, silver, copper, and oil, which need to be discovered before they can be drawn from the ground, so, too, organizations contain vast, untapped human resources. We need to perfect the art and science of human interaction to realize our potential more fully.

Our formulation is cast in the positive. Let me try saying the same thing, but in the negative. The misuse of human resources in some of our organizations rivals the exploitation of the environment during the past hundred years. In some cases, the destruction of human resources is simply a result of their overuse by forcing people to do more and more in less and less time. In some cases, outright exploitation, if understood fully, would become a crime against humanity. The toll of overwork and under-appreciation on individuals, family life, relationships, and health cannot be fully quantified, but it is enormous. We need to wake up to the human suffering endured by so many under the dictatorship of King Dollar.

Key words for Jupiter-style leadership:
grand vision, creative thoughts, vigor

The Mars Type

Whereas the Jupiter type seeks to convince, Mars-type leaders persuade. Jupiter may hold back until the moment is ripe for their inspirational vision, but Mars leaders are comfortable participating actively throughout the process. Mars types love to share, talk, and persuade. They engage with great zest and fervor. Any topic is of interest as long as it can be brought into debate and discussion. These types make great lawyers and public speakers.

Mars leaders have long been pioneers, because they have a sort of fearless attitude toward the unknown. They will go where none have gone before, navigating across unknown seas, developing new technologies, and trying out new ideas. Questioning assumptions comes naturally. They can inspire others to follow and rally the troops, even when the cause seems hopeless. Thus, many famous generals have been Mars-type leaders. Today, many of these individuals are found in the ranks of CEOs of pioneering companies, developing and conquering new markets and forging ahead.

Mars types are willing to take responsibility for their actions and to be held accountable. However, they expect the same of others around them, and can appear ruthless and arbitrary when groups are indecisive and weak. They are natural leaders and can become frustrated when others dither. They need to channel their zest into forming articulate arguments rather than forcing resolution through dint of personality. Persuasion is thus an art form that can engage the latent energy of Mars.

Ability with words is a talent and certainly preferable to the use of force. Language requires both form and content, and when a Mars type is paired with a Venus type, wonderful things can emerge. Great writers are often fed by both Venus and Mars, the art and formation of language. If you study the human larynx, you can see a physical manifestation of consonants and vowels, the form and the feeling. Both are needed in speech.

When working with Mars leaders in an organization, job assignments are crucial. You do not want to give Mars types routine, clerical tasks. This will cause them to apply all their ingenuity to finding ways of avoiding doing the task themselves. Mars types need to feel a sense of adventure, forging new ground, discovering, and exploring, even if it means just doing something in a new way. Give Mars types leadership roles, but balance them with people who draw from the other planets. If there are difficulties, engage and discuss. The worst thing is to leave the Mars type alone, deprived of human interaction. They feed off conversation and debate and need the challenge of listening and talking as a means of self-development.

Owing to their checkered history of violent solutions to world problems, Mars types may have accumulated a bad rap. I would like to urge those who work with groups and organizations to reimagine the wonderful potential of Mars leaders. We need their inspirational qualities, their willingness to *move beyond the status quo*, and their unshakable faith in human potential. In an age when everything can be easily reduced to the "bottom line" and when hard, unshakable facts often depress and rule our thinking, Mars leaders can sometimes lift us out of our lethargy and help us see new horizons. Especially as our schools and businesses age with time, we have to beware of "stealth Saturnization"; we need Mars to reenergize and awaken consciousness. Like the massive Ents in Tolkein's *Lord of the Rings,* humanity can easily fall asleep and become all bark. We can counter such hardening of human nature both through crises (such as the burning of the forests in *Return of the King*) and through consciously awakening through active inner development, research, innovation, and enlivening conversation.

Key words for Mars-style leadership:
persuade, engage, explore, forge ahead, question the
status quo, find new solutions to old problems, lead

The Venus Type

Leadership comes naturally to Mars types, but it is not so obvious with Venus. In fact, Venus types can be difficult to approach, because they try to preserve some of their intrinsic nature for purposes other than formal leadership. They have a strong aesthetic sense and love to transform earthly experiences into dream pictures through art. One might say that the Venus leader is an artist. Venus types see beauty as an end in itself and value the process and the product equally. Great poets, painters, and dancers have the remarkable ability to take common earthly experiences and lift them to a level that brings nobility, refinement, and dignity to humanity. Venus types can lift the commonplace to a higher level through artistry.

Venus-oriented people help us to learn from life. They are able to take the ordinary experiences that we all go through and lift them to thought images that become lessons in life. When this happens in a group, experiences are objectified. This means that we can see them together instead of splintering off into separate personalities. The common picture unites what had been separate.

A Venus leader I observed a few years ago was marvelously adept at painting pictures with words, speaking in rich images that nourish the soul. She was thoroughly artistic, working with the raw material of human resources through personal conversation and her deep interest in the striving of others. However, eventually she was criticized for not being decisive enough, postponing difficult decisions, and working in elliptical patterns. She was replaced by a more traditional leader, with the result that many of those in the organization who had been nourished by her efforts soon became demoralized.

The New England birch tree represents much that is associated with the Venus type. Often slender and striking in its white bark, the birch accents the dark forest. It often grows in clusters and is easily damaged in a winter storm. Indeed, the birch does not live as long as many other trees, sometimes only thirty years or less. Nevertheless, it graces the environment with its beauty and delicacy.

It is important for groups to protect and support the Venus types so they can make their contribution to the process of life and growth. Transformative work is selfless, but at the same time essential for human progress.

Key words for Venus types: artistic,
transformative, sensitive, pictorial

The Mercury Type

Coordination is the aspect of leadership that best characterizes the Mercury impulse. These folks are adept at connecting people with one another, juggling multiple tasks, and smoothing things over. They are able to do this with a keen intellect and a remarkable ability to connect the dots. They use reason and people skills to weave between different dynamics and help various personalities work together.

An excellent example of the Mercury style is often found in hospitals. Weaving among the many "I" beings on the medical staff, one finds nurses who coordinate the ins and outs of patient care to make things work. I have been impressed with how many nurses can multitask, coordinate specialists, and adapt their manner to the patient or doctor at hand. This adaptation is a crucial skill in large organizations, and the Mercury types often hold the whole enterprise together.

These coordinators often live in the moment. Like jugglers, Mercury types have to be fully present to keep everything on track. Their people skills are often called on in a way that requires a refined sense of which way the wind is blowing, knowing what to say and when. Many of the

Mercury leaders I have known are exceptionally good at choosing their words and using what we call tact. Many are diplomats.

These talents also come with a price. It is hard to get Mercury types to take initiative. They see initiative as belonging to others such as the Jupiter and Mars types. Yet if organizations are to grow or remain relevant, they need new programs and products. At best, one can ask Mercury leaders to coordinate meetings that would draw out the innovative ideas of others. They will encourage and support the process during meetings, but afterward they will become fully present with some other situation and may not follow through with more than reporting.

Indeed, Mercury types are good communicators, but they are also quick to move on to other things and need to be reminded repeatedly about organizational priorities. Communicating is necessary, but not sufficient for many tasks.

Although I respect the need for clear communication, over the years I have grown wary of putting too much emphasis on simply reporting. Often an assumption lives in the workplace that if we simply communicate well, everything else will take care of itself.

I feel similarly about the constant call for transparency. What does that really mean? Physical things cannot be fully transparent, but ideas can be shared in a way that sheds light through them so that others can make them their own. In a report, it is possible to take the listeners through a process in such a way that they experience, vicariously perhaps, the major turning points along the way. This creates a possible foundation for what is called "buy in."

However, no organization can be truly transparent and still exist. In some ways, one might call an over-emphasis on communication and transparency a death wish. Living organisms are inherently mysterious, and some of the most remarkable processes require the cloak of opaqueness to really flourish. For example, where does an initiative come from? How can one be fully aware of the sources of inspiration? These aspects are deeply spiritual and need to be cradled opaquely in a kind of womb of during gestation. The demand for immediate and open communication can hinder a magical process that may not be understood fully until much later.

Another way of saying this is that too much consciousness can kill a living impulse. A plant would never grow just with light; it needs the darkness of the damp earth, as well. Too much light can deprive living things of the nurturing impulse. But if we live with something long enough, higher wisdom can gradually dawn.

Being so adept at living in the here-and-now, Mercury types need to grow increasingly respectful of life's greater mysteries that take time to unfold. Such growing appreciation may come with age and experience and with a growing awareness that all of these styles of leadership are interdependent. The ultimate goal of modern-day leadership is therefore a newfound affirmation of the group—not blind, touchy-feely, group stuff, but a clear awareness of the majestic tapestry of intertwined leadership.

Key words for Mercury-style leadership:
coordination, diplomacy, communication

The Sun Type

Wisdom and Sun leadership seem to go hand-in-hand. Certain people seem to radiate warmth and benevolence, and the world is a better place because of their presence. These special people may have formal roles through which to dispense their advice—gurus, rabbis, priests, or elders to whom people turn with life questions. Yet fortunately for our civilization, there are some who are also informal Sun leaders—grandparents, faithful friends, special teachers, or neighbors. Such individuals radiate goodwill and sage advice.

Because they create harmony among different impulses, Sun leaders are often surrounded by people seeking resolution to one problem or another. For example, there may be tension in a person's life between freedom and necessity—what was given through heredity, career, and family, and what slumbers under the heart as an unfulfilled wish. It is part of our modern condition that people can feel trapped between what they long to do and what they have to do. Such a one could be a mid-career person who earns well but wants to do something more rewarding that may carry financial and other risks. How can we navigate between these conflicting impulses?

Sun leaders are often helpful in weaving between destiny and freedom, connecting the threads that have been invisible until that crucial conversation. Through their warmth and deep human interest, Sun leaders can help people resolve destiny into freedom. They generally refrain from telling a person what to do and instead, through their manner of speech and guided conversation, help a person discover a way through the maze of a turning point. Such an encounter often leads to a profound sense of joy.

These wise counselors would seem to have no shadow sides, yet as with all leaders, there is at least one. Because Sun leaders have achieved such inner harmony, they tend to be somewhat self-sufficient and self-contained. They repose in the harmony of body and soul, and therefore can sometimes be impervious to the turmoil and struggle around them. They have been known to hold back occasionally and fail to intervene when needed. It is a rare thing to be both wise and appropriately active, swooping in like Gandalf when needed while still allowing others to evolve freely. Sun leaders need to practice active perception and not rely only on Sun wisdom of the past.

Key words for Sun style leadership:
harmony, wisdom, inner contentment

Situational Leadership

One of the drawbacks of any typology such as the planetary leadership styles is that people may feel "pegged" into one category or another. This can happen, for example, with Meyers-Briggs Type Indicator learning styles or with any other system of classifying human beings in a schematic way. However, what is essential is the learning tools that we can bring to bear in concrete life situations. The planetary leadership styles are intended as pathways to greater self-awareness and effectiveness in the workplace. Nevertheless, we do not need to look at any single style exclusively. Rather, they become truly interesting when we can apply them situationally.

Rather than merely determining one's own planetary style, it is helpful to observe the constellation of a group and adapt accordingly. Indeed, all of the planetary modalities work in each of us, though some will predominate. Thus, if we observe a strong Saturn influence in the group, we can look at balancing possibilities. Rather than coming on strong with Mars or Jupiter, we may find that encouraging Venus or Mercury will get things moving out of the past and into the present. Likewise, a strong Mars influence can be helped by expanding consciousness into the big picture work of Jupiter. Knowing what is needed depends on both perception and intuition.

This then leads to the question: How can I develop my abilities so that I can better perceive and then act in a way that is most helpful to the situation? There is a great deal of material on self-development, so I would like to indicate one meditative practice that builds on the material relating to the planets. Ancient scholars knew that the days of the week are connected to the cosmos—that Tuesday, for example, is a Mars day. In fact, each day of the week can be associated with a specific planet.

Monday	Moon
Tuesday	Mars
Wednesday	Mercury
Thursday	Jupiter
Friday	Venus
Saturday	Saturn
Sunday	Sun

If we live through a week and sense the different qualities of each day, we may begin to sense the planetary influences. For example, we may find that we relate to certain days in a more positive way than we do to others. This is a very individual process and can change with different periods of life.

This gets really exciting when we begin an active meditative practice in relation to the different days of the week, using the hidden potential of each day for personal self-development. This makes it possible to be the person on needs to be in a given life situation. Instead of responding in one's preferred or comfortable modality, we respond in the way that is helpful to the situation—the *kairos,* the right time and day.

Monday	Right Word
Tuesday	Right Deed
Wednesday	Right Standpoint/Perspective
Thursday	Let all the exercises become habitual
Friday	Right Memory
Saturday	Right Opinion
Sunday	Right Judgment [13]

The practice of these exercises helps us live more fully in each moment of the day. For example, knowing when to speak and when to hold back requires a special kind of presence. Often, I have realized only afterward that I should have said something; or I may regret speaking too soon. The Monday exercise of right word is a kind of awareness that calls for us to give or hold back, engage or not. Do I share what is within me or should I preserve it for another time? This dilemma is associated with the Moon quality of preserved wisdom finding its right relation to present conditions.

---

13. Steiner, *Guidance in Esoteric Training,* pp. 20–21. Material in appendix 1 describes in more detail these contemplative practices indicated by Rudolf Steiner in relation to the days of the week.

By living in full attentiveness through the gesture of the day, we can exercise better situational leadership. We often think of leadership as just "doing things" (the Mars, or Tuesday, orientation). But this is like just living one day of the week, or eating only one kind of food. Leadership is more than acting in the outer sense; it comes in multiple forms. Speaking can be a form of leadership, not only the inspirational sort of speech, but also simply finding the right words to say in a given situation. A few words can change the whole dynamic of a group, for better or worse. To take another example, finding the right judgment is crucial for leaders. Going through a process of "reasoned deliberation" is crucial to forming a judgment on an issue. The question to leaders is often: Where do you stand on this issue? What is said out of reasoned deliberation can make a huge difference in the course of events.

The tricky part is that we cannot plan all of our actions, words, and judgments ahead to time. One has to live in the moment and bring to each situation the very best one has to offer. This is situational leadership.

Meditative practices help us develop the mindfulness and the inner resources from which we exercise leadership in the moment. Those who have found an inner orientation develop a deep respect for the enormity of the spiritual world around us. We live not surrounded just by houses, plants, and people, but also by spiritual influences that are generally invisible but just as real as the material things we see and touch. The intangible resources of the spiritual world are available to those who open themselves accordingly.

Working with the days of the week and other exercises develops the ability to be truly present in a situation. Then, out of that presence, one can take hold of an impulse and bring it into the world, either through an action, a word, or a formulation of judgment. This basic sharing of inner resources is a leadership deed for humanity. If we take a leadership role, even for a few moments in a certain situation, we have opened a channel, or vehicle, for spiritual impulses to flow into the world. *Situational leadership is focused energy and insight, exercised in the moment, on behalf of a group, organization, or human situation.* We spiritualize Earth through our initiative and leadership.

Speaking of Earth, one can say in simple terms that the heavy, dark, sense-bound entity we call Earth is often foremost in our consciousness these days. We tend to orient ourselves toward the phenomena we can experience sensorially; we spend many years trying to satisfy perceived needs. Yet we are not just creatures of Earth. Each person has a source of light within. It can at times be darkened, but is nevertheless always present. Leaders need to work with that spark that resides in each human being, seeing the potential in others and carrying a hopeful attitude toward what resides as inner wisdom. We need to reclaim that inner spark again and again if it is not to be submerged in the materialism of the earthly world. Giving credence and acknowledgement to the light pole in human nature is an essential task of leaders. It can be as little as a timely smile, words spoken in compassion, or a thoughtful deed. If we do not attend to our humanity, no one else will.

I am the decisive element

I have come to the frightening conclusion that
    I am the decisive element.
It is my personal approach that creates the climate.
    It is my daily mood that makes the weather.
    I possess tremendous power to make life
    miserable or joyous.
I can be a tool of torture or an instrument of
    inspiration; I can humiliate or humor, hurt
    or heal. In all situations, it is my response
    that decides whether a crisis is escalated or
    de-escalated, and a person is humanized or
    de-humanized.
If we treat people as they are, we make them worse.
    If we treat people as they ought to be, we help
    them become what they are capable of becoming.
                (generally attributed to J. W. Goethe)

Planetary Influences at Different Phases in Life

Many psychologists have described life phases (Erikson, Kagan, Piaget). They have certain common features that make life more intelligible. Although each human biography is of course unique, the concept of life phases gives us information on how particular individuals are negotiating the intricate journey between form and freedom— between what is given and what arises through free choice. By studying life phases, we can see the whole human being unfolding in patterns that become visible over time. Likewise, our self-development and what we do in life is very much connected to the archetypal phases of life.

Near the end of his life in 1924, Rudolf Steiner made several references to his age in relation to planetary

*The universe depicted in Buch der Natur (1350),
showing a hierarchy of the elements, planetary
spheres, and the Christian heaven*

influences. For instance, "In actual vision it is possible to behold these happenings and their connections only when one has passed the sixty-third year of life…the Saturn existence."[14] In this section, I would like to explore in more detail why he would make such a comment and how the phases of life are related to the different planets and shape leadership potential.

---

14. Quoted in O'Neil, *The Human Life*, p. 102.

Life periods are windows into the wider world, helping us objectify our own experiences and rendering them transparent so that we can take up our tasks in a new way. Likewise, these windows let the influences of the outer world, including the planets, stream into our inner being. Just as our state of mind is influenced by the gorgeous sunny day or incessant rain and fog, so also the planets speak to human beings differently in the various periods of life.

The Knights Templar of the Middle Ages had a flag that showed how a human life on Earth is a journey from the Moon to Saturn. In a more detailed drawing (next page), one can represent the human birth at the center (each birth is the creation of a new world) and the corresponding rings of life phases unfolding in space and time.

What do these planetary life periods mean in terms of human biography? Here are some key words for each:

Moon phase, from birth to age seven: birth, family, heredity, childlike fantasy and image making, gradual transformation of physical body into instrument that serves the particular individual

Mercury phase, ages seven to fourteen: golden years of childhood, rich imagination, vitality and energy, zest for learning, interest in many things/natural curiosity, sanguine

Venus phase, ages fourteen to twenty-one: emerging sense of self, tremendous physical changes, love of beauty, attraction to others, idealism

Sun phase, ages twenty-one to forty-two: independence of self, individuality begins to shine, initiative and responsibility ripen, maturity now more of an inner process/less visible outwardly

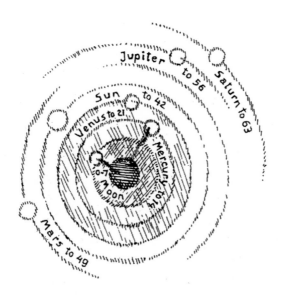

Mars phase, ages forty-two to forty-nine: strong individu-
alization, further definition or redefinition of career,
active outwardly, taking on of personal and professional
responsibilities

Jupiter phase, ages forty-nine to fifty-six: growing wisdom
and breadth of overview, willingness to take on larger
tasks, sense of confidence and certainty after midlife
changes

Saturn phase, ages fifty-six to sixty-three: more bound by
hard realities of life experiences and memories, yet at the
same time willing to serve selflessly, less bound by physical constraints, more willing to simply do what is right.[15]

Looking at the overview of life phases, it is fascinating to observe leaders from this point of view. What a
difference it makes if someone is serving at a youthful
twenty-eight or at the mature age of sixty. Often, we

---

15. These insights are from George and Gisela O'Neil, *The
Human Life,* pp 109–110.

draw our formal leaders from the ranks of people aged fifty-six to sixty-three, without much knowledge of the opportunities and challenges that come during that life phase. For example, the strong administrative bent of many modern-day organizations is owed in part to the nature of leaders from the Saturn period. In contrast, most innovative businesses such as start-up companies are led in their initial phase by much younger people. Both impulses are needed in a healthy organization, and the challenge is finding ways to integrate the different planetary streams into a harmonious order.

Several thousand years ago, the great Indian sages where known for their profound wisdom; they were teachers in the greatest sense of the word. They matured throughout life, with their soul capacities developing alongside the maturation of the physical body until the fifty-sixth year. After that age, self-development and specific spiritual practices were needed to continue with the soul's development. Otherwise, the physical body would mature without any corresponding further development of the soul capacities. Thus, many in Indian culture put great emphasis on Yoga, or the attunement of the soul, which has been handed down to countless generations in the years that followed.

Later on, the concurrent soul-physical development would last only until the forty-ninth year; this occurred during the flowering of ancient Persian culture. Then, during the time of the ancient Egyptians, the simultaneous development of soul and body occurred only until the forty-second year. After that time, it was up to each individual whether to freely take up a path of self-development or not. At the time of the ancient Greeks and Romans, soul development ended at the relatively youthful age of thirty-five, and today we are closer to the age of twenty-seven.[16]

What this means is that, for those who do not take up further inner development, their body matures past age twenty-seven while the soul remains relatively immature. We see many adult men and women who seem to want to remain perpetually in their twenties, even into midlife. This has profound implications for the ways we work together and how we view leadership.

As mentioned, each life phase has a planetary gesture. So it makes a great difference whether someone is working out of a Venus impulse or one of Saturn. In fact, many of our organizations are lead by outwardly mature individuals who still have the emotional, soul life of an earlier stage. This leads to seemingly endless reoccurrences of old patterns of behavior as groups try and break out of the planetary trap of one-sided influences. For example, we might have many people in an organization who, inwardly, are still in the hands-on, lets-do-it-together gesture of the Sun period, while the formal leader might be in his or her sixties, with more of an "old world" approach to organizational matters. The issues might change from month to month, but when we see the dynamic occur repeatedly, forming an organizational pattern, we have to take another look at both the people and the life stages involved.

Through conscious self-development and focused exercises, it is possible to take one's own life path in hand and move gracefully through the planetary stages, gleaning the wonderful wisdom available through each stage and

16. Steiner, *Aspects of Human Evolution*, pp. 4–8.

forming a deep reservoir of collected life experience that can result in true situational leadership—being who one needs to be given the situation at hand. Thus, the more we involve people who have developed in this way, the more effective we become in fulfilling our life tasks and the aims of our organizations.

Conclusion: Volunteerism

One form of leadership not often identified or even fully appreciated are the numerous volunteers who serve in various capacities in most local communities. I recently had an opportunity to address a group of teachers, parents, and board members at an advisory board meeting of the Pine Hill Waldorf School on precisely this aspect of servant leadership:

> Looking at the local towns around our school, we see not-for-profit organizations that often are the heart and soul of community interactions: the local library, museum, theater, independent school, farmers' market, volunteer ambulance service, and so on. Good people with a variety of professional backgrounds step forward to serve, often after hours and despite family constraints. Yet I cannot recall hearing of any of these groups receiving the kind of "stimulus" money that went to General Motors or Citibank...nonprofits seem to have been almost forgotten by our political leaders, yet they are the ones that often hold a community together. Volunteerism is especially important in terms of the cultural life of a community; one might say the heart and soul of our local surroundings.

Those of us who are volunteers are called to serve out of the deep folds of idealism. Unlike those who receive a monthly paycheck, however small it may be, or even those who are trustees with a vote that can have at least a passing shred of control, true volunteers serve out of intrinsic values with no form of recompense. We serve not just for the sake of the institutions that draw us together, but also out of a deep-seated desire to grow as human beings. Volunteerism assists in personal development. We learn, grow, and develop new capacities through our community work. What may have been incomplete can become whole thanks to working with others. We can become more than we have been thanks to our service.

One of the reasons for this has to do with the passage of time. In a world where test scores and profit-and-loss statements value only the here and now, volunteering for non-profits is an investment in the long-term future. SATs may measure a math ability today, but what our children receive in a Waldorf school may not manifest fully for ten, twenty, thirty, or more years. One has to believe in the future of humanity in order to work for a nonprofit.

What are the resources out of which one can volunteer? We need to cultivate inner substantiality so that the fountainhead of our volunteerism can be renewed continually. Of course, there are many paths for such inner renewal, and it is a profound matter of personal freedom to decide which path to choose. However, I urge volunteers to attend to replenishment.

Here is a simple example of how one might call on the ideals that lend support:

Help me
Become the person I have always longed to be.
Give me the strength to serve,
And the knowledge to know where I am needed
The perception to step forward when the time is right
And the tact to withdraw when the job is done.

May I be true to my ideals
Flexible in the ebb and flow of daily life
Yet unswerving in upholding the truth.
May I find joy in my interactions with others
And practice kindness in the face of our mutual
    shortcomings.

Help me see the eternal in each human being
Thus releasing the goodness that this world so
    desperately needs.
I offer myself as an instrument
Of the higher intentions of this school.
For I believe in the future.

~

EPILOGUE

As the reader may have noticed throughout this book, I based all my research on an anthroposophic worldview as described by Rudolf Steiner in numerous books and lectures. In all my books, I have tried to use the methods indicated by Anthroposophy to explore the themes they covered, because it is the path of inquiry that has proven most helpful. Anthroposophy has also helped me think creatively, to see the world with fresh eyes, and to explore in deeply satisfying ways. Without this creative impulse, I could not have found my writer's voice, nor indeed would I have had much to say at all.

I am mindful that this particular book is published in 2011, a year that marks the 150th anniversary of Rudolf Steiner's birth. Thus, it is especially appropriate that I acknowledge my spiritual resources and the founder of Anthroposophy.

During a time of inner preparation at the start of this significant year, from December 25 to January 6, I reread many of the accounts of Steiner's life and work. As I read the various books in my collection, I asked myself the simple question: Who was Rudolf Steiner? Then something interesting happened—the question changed. On the weekend of January 6, I found myself asking: Who *is* Rudolf Steiner?

As I took my musings out into conversations with friends, groups, and branches of the Anthroposophical Society, I found that the dialogue had expanded on several levels. There were of course the conversations among friends, but also their conversations with the works and citations I brought into the meetings. Often, however, as things progressed, there was a sense of addressing the man himself, and people shared some intimate experiences of their connection with Rudolf Steiner. At times, it was as if we were calling on him in his 150th year.

Then, one morning I awoke in my home in Temple, New Hampshire, with a strong impulse after having lived with the transformed question of "Who *is* Rudolf Steiner?" It led me to rush down to my desk that morning and write a verse, something I have rarely done. It was as though I had been called out of sleep early that morning to write *to* the person who has inspired so much of my life work. I simply obeyed the impulse and scribbled some lines down on a piece of paper.

Afterward, I felt somewhat shocked. Who am I to write to this remarkable man? However, after sharing it with my dear wife, Karine, and then later with a friend who helped with some editing, I decided it had happened for a reason and typed it up. Since then, I have read it at the conclusion of several celebratory events for Rudolf Steiner's 150th anniversary. I feel it might also serve as a fitting conclusion to this book.

On the 150th Anniversary
of Rudolf Steiner's Birth: 1861–2011

O Seeker
Champion of the Spirit,
Servant of humanity!

Help us continue the work that you began,
Fulfilling the promise of a living Anthroposophy.
You showed us the way:
We are not bound by necessity of natural laws.
Rather, the human being, spiritually free
Through self-directed thinking,
Can forge a new organ of perception and cross the divide
Between a world of the senses and the supersensible.
Human beings can develop moral insight
    that leads to moral action.

O Seeker
Help us remember to lift our gaze to the horizon
To see what is truly important.
Too often, we fall back into our petty selves, divisions,
    and self-will.
Help us seek, know, and perceive the eternal
    in each human being
At every street corner.
And help us summon up compassion for our shortcomings,
Forgiveness for past conflicts,
For often, we know not what we do.

Champion of the Spirit
We begin to appreciate the personal pain of the teacher
Only when his students fail their lessons.
It is part of the struggle of our time
To begin, and then have to begin again,

Always renewing faith in the ultimate goal
To emerge after the long age of darkness
Into the light of spirit wakefulness.

We are dedicated
To the tasks you set before us
Humbled
In the knowledge of what has not yet been accomplished
Yet emboldened
By the courage of your incarnations.

Servant of humanity!
On this day we pledge
To work collaboratively, consciously, and courageously
For spirit awakening and the heart's power of love.
We work with the unifying presence of Michael
As part of a worldwide movement
Of cultural renewal

Forging ahead with clarity,
Feeling our common humanity,
Deepening our compassion,
Strengthening our sense of purpose
With self-responsible, self-directed willing.

Torin M. Finser
February 2011

APPENDIX 1:
MEDITATIONS FOR
THE DAYS OF THE WEEK

Saturday

To pay attention to one's ideas.

To think only significant thoughts. To learn little by little to separate in one's thoughts the essential from the nonessential, the eternal from the transitory, truth from mere opinion.

Listening to the talk of one's companions, to try to become quite still inwardly, foregoing all assent, and still more all unfavorable judgments (criticism, rejection), even in one's thoughts and feelings. This may be called *right opinion*.

Sunday

To decide on even the most insignificant matter only after fully reasoned deliberation. All unthinking behavior, all meaningless actions, should be kept far away from the soul. One should definitely abstain from doing anything for which there is no significant reason.

Once one is convinced of the rightness of a decision, one must hold fast to it, with inner steadfastness.

This may be called *right judgment*, having been formed independently of sympathies and antipathies.

Monday

Talking. Only what has sense and meaning should come from the lips of one striving for higher development. All talking for the sake of talking—to kill time—is in this sense harmful.

The usual kind of conversation, a disjointed medley of remarks, should be avoided. This does not mean shutting oneself off from interactions with others. It is precisely then that talk should gradually be led to significance. One adopts a thoughtful attitude to every speech and answer, taking all aspects into account. Never talk without cause— be gladly silent. One tries not to talk too much or too little. First listen quietly; then reflect on what has been said. This exercise may be called **right word**.

Tuesday

External actions. These should not be disturbing for those around us. When an occasion calls for action from one's inner being, deliberate carefully how one can best meet the occasion—for the good of the whole, the lasting happiness of man, the eternal. Where one does things of one's own accord, out of one's own initiative: consider most thoroughly beforehand the effect of one's actions. This is called **right deed.**

Wednesday

The ordering of life. To live in accordance with nature and spirit. Not to be swamped by the external trivialities of life. To avoid all that brings unrest and haste into life. To hurry over nothing, but also not to be indolent. To look on life as a means for working toward higher development and to behave accordingly. One speaks in this connection of *right standpoint*.

Thursday

Human Endeavor. One should take care to do nothing that lies beyond one's powers—but also to leave nothing undone which lies within them. To look beyond the everyday, the momentary, and to set oneself aims and ideals connected with the highest duties of a human being. For instance, in the sense of the prescribed exercises, to try to develop oneself so that afterward one may be able to help all the more and advise others—though perhaps not in the immediate future.

This can be summed up as *"Let all the foregoing exercises become a habit."*

Friday

The endeavor to learn as much as possible from life. Nothing goes by us without giving us a chance to gain experiences that are useful for life. If one has done something wrongly or imperfectly, that becomes a motive for doing it rightly or more perfectly later on.

If one sees others doing something, one observes them with the like end in view (yet, not coldly or heartlessly). And one does nothing without looking back to past experiences that can be of assistance in one's decisions and achievements.

One can learn from everyone—even from children if one is attentive. This exercise is called *right memory* (remembering what has been learned from experiences).

Summary

To turn one's gaze inward from time to time, even if only for five minutes daily at the same time. In so doing one should sink into oneself, carefully take counsel with oneself, test and form one's principles of life, run through in thought one's knowledge—or lack of it—weigh up one's duties, think over the contents and true purpose of life, feel genuinely pained by one's own errors and imperfections. In other words, labor to discover the essential and enduring and earnestly aim at goals in accord with it—for instance, virtues to be acquired. Try not to fall into the mistake of thinking one has done something well, but strive ever further toward the highest standards.

This exercise is called *right examination*.

❧

APPENDIX 2:
THE PENTAGRAM AS A TOOL
FOR SELF-DEVELOPMENT

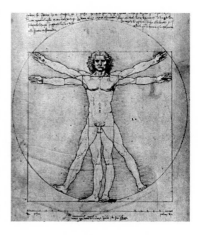

If one delves further into the mystery of the pentagram mentioned earlier in this book, one can find one gem after another. For example, ancient wisdom often contains reference to earth, air, fire, and water as alchemical ingredients that can be brought into harmony through the efforts of the striving human being. Each element was believed to be filled with life force, and these could be arranged on the self-same pentagram (next page). Indeed, one finds the five-pointed star in nature in numerous flowers, as well as in the essential form of the human being with outstretched arms and legs.

When the pentagram is inverted and the point is down, one has a symbol long associated with dark magic and with those seeking power for personal gain. Conversely, when turned right-side up again, the pentagram is featured in the church blessing practiced by many Christians today—using the hand to outline a five-pointed star, from the head down to the right, up to the left, across the body, down to

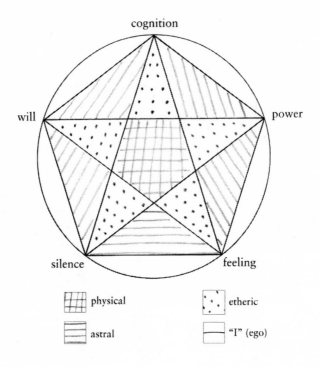

the left, and back to the center. In many denominations, it is the priest who can then do one more motion—the completed circle around the whole star. Here, we have again the circle representing the higher element, the "I."

The following table draws together many of the concepts and elements discussed throughout this book.

PLANET	Moon	Mars	Mercury	Jupiter	Venus	Saturn	Sun
DAY	Monday	Tuesday	Wednesday	Thursday	Friday	Saturday	Sunday
SYMBOL	☽	♂	☿	♃	♀	♄	☉
COLOR	lilac, peach blossom	red	yellow	orange	green	dark blue	white, light blue
METAL	silver	iron	mercury	tin	copper	lead	gold
WOOD	fruit-trees	oak	elm	maple	birch	pine	ash
GRAIN	rice	oats	millet	rye	barley	corn	wheat
ORGAN	glands	gallbladder	lungs	liver	kidney	spleen	heart
CYCLE	ages 0–7	ages 42–49	ages 7–14	ages 49–56	ages 14–21	ages 56–63	ages 21–42
ARCHANGEL	Gabriel	Samael	Raphael	Zerachiel	Anael (Uriel)	Oriphael	Michael
INFLUENCE	life forces, growth, propagation	strength, energy	sociability, interaction	overview	beauty, love	responsibility	healing wisdom
ACTIVITY	baking bread	building, gardening	eurythmy, drama	crafts	painting, beeswax	cleaning	stories, music

❧

APPENDIX 3:
FROM THE ANTHROPOSOPHICAL
PRISON OUTREACH PROGRAM

I recently found yet a further confirmation of the transcendant in *Illuminating Anthroposophy: The Anthroposophical Prison Outreach Newsletter*. The issue reprinted a letter from an inmate in Texas:

> I would like to share what has happened to me since I started my spiritual journey through Anthroposophy. I have only been involved now for two years, but I have seen nothing but positive results in my life. I am not the only one to see these results as many inmates have asked me about my change. As time passes, I have become aware how my emotions, my intuition, and my spirit have come to balance out more in my life. It is no longer about myself, but about others. It is about evolving to become a better person to make this earth a better place to live in, not only for the people of now, but also for the next generations to come. My confidence level is up again. Now I know I am some-one important on this vast universe. I can finally say that I can see myself from the outside in.[1]

---

1. Issue 15, p. 5, winter/spring 2011.

REFERENCES AND FURTHER READING

Adams, George. *The Mysteries of the Rose Cross*, London: Temple Lodge, 1989.

Bennel, Margaret. and Isabel Wyatt, *A Commentary on The Chymical Wedding of Christian Rosenkreutz, Anno 1459*. Gloucester, UK: The Michael Press, n.d.

Ben Aharon, Jesaiah. *The New Experience of the Supersensible: The Anthroposophical Knowledge Drama of Our Time*, London: Temple Lodge, 2007.

Bittleston, Adam. *The Seven Planets*, Oxford, UK: Floris Books, 1985.

Chopra, Deepak, ed. *The Love Poems of Rumi*, New York: Harmony, 1998.

Deresiewicz, William. "Solitude and Leadership," *Utne Reader*, Sep.–Oct. 2010.

Emerson, Ralph Waldo, *Essays*, New York: Three Sirens Press, c. 1932.

Drucker, Peter, F. *Innovation and Entrepreneurship*, New York: HarperCollins, 1986.

Finser, Torin. *Organizational Integrity: How to Apply the Wisdom of the Body to Develop Healthy Organizations*, Great Barrington, MA: Anthroposophic Press, 2007.

———. *School Renewal: A Spiritual Journey for Change*, Great Barrington, MA: Anthroposophic Press, 2001.

Grimm's Fairy Tales, Margaret Hunt, trans., New York: Random House, 1972.

Hamilton, Edith. *Mythology: Timeless Tales of Gods and Heroes*, New York: Warner, 1942.

Himmelsbach, L., J. Hemleben, and Norbert Thomsen. *Besinnung zu Den Wochentagen*, Görwihl, Germany: Liselotte Himmelsbach.

Meadows, Donella, H. *Thinking in Systems: A Primer*, White River Junction, VT: Chelsea Green, 2008.

O'Neil, George, and Gisela O'Neil. *The Human Life*, NY: Mercury Press, 1990.

Peace Pilgrim. *Peace Pilgrim: Her Life and Work in Her Own Words*, Santa Fe, NM: Ocean Tree, 1981.

Pelikan, Wilhelm. *The Secrets of Metals*, Great Barrington, MA: SteinerBooks, 2006.

Pfeiffer, Ehrenfried. E., *The Chymical Wedding of Christian Rosenkreutz*, Spring Valley, NY: Mercury, 1984.

Sease, Virginia, and Manfred Schmidt-Brabant, *Paths of the Christian Mysteries: From Compostela to the New World*, London: Temple Lodge, 2003.

Steiner, Rudolf. *Aspects of Human Evolution*, Hudson, NY: Anthroposophic Press, 1987.

———. *Christian Rosenkreutz: The Mystery, Teaching and Mission of a Master*, London: Sophia Books, 2001.

———. *Esoteric Christianity: and the Mission of Christian Rosenkreutz*, London: Rudolf Steiner Press, 2005.

———. *Goethe's Theory of Knowledge: An Outline of the Epistemology of His Worldview*, Great Barrington, MA: SteinerBooks, 2008.

———. *Guidance in Esoteric Training: From the Esoteric School*, London: Rudolf Steiner Press, 2001.

———. *Introducing Anthroposophical Medicine*, Great Barrington, MA: SteinerBooks, 2010.

———. *Intuitive Thinking as a Spiritual Path: A Philosophy of Freedom*, Hudson, NY: Anthroposophic Press, 1995.

———. Lecture, Berlin, June 26, 1906 (typescript).

———. "Man as a Picture of the Living Spirit" (lecture, Sept. 2, 1923), London: Rudolf Steiner Press, 1972.

———. *Old and New Methods of Initiation*, London: Rudolf Steiner Press, 1991.

———. *The Presence of the Dead on the Spiritual Path*, Hudson, NY: Anthroposophic Press, 1990.

———. *A Psychology of Body, Soul, and Spirit: Anthroposophy, Psychosophy, Pneumatosophy*, Hudson, NY: Anthroposophic Press, 1999.

————. *Rosicrucian Wisdom: An Introduction*, London: Rudolf
  Steiner Press, 2005.

————. *The Stages of Higher Knowledge: Imagination, Inspiration,
  Intuition*, Great Barrington, MA: SteinerBooks, 2009.

————. *Truth-Wrought-Words and Other Verses*, Spring Valley, NY:
  Anthroposophic Press, 1979.

————. *Wonders of the World, Ordeals of the Soul, Revelations of
  the Spirit*, London: Rudolf Steiner Press, 1963.

Stibbe, Max. *Seven Soul Types*, Stroud, UK: Hawthorn Press, 1992.

Thoreau, Henry, *Walden*, South San Francisco: Long River, 1976.

von Goethe, Johann Wolfgang. *Theory of Colors*, Cambridge, MA:
  M.I.T., 1987.

von Halle, Judith. *And if He Had Not Been Raised...: The Stations
  of Christ's Path to Spirit Man*, London: Temple Lodge, 2007.

Ward, William. *Traveling Light: Walking the Cancer Path*, Great
  Barrington, MA: Lindisfarne Books, 2007.

Wolff, Otto. *The Etheric Body*, Spring Valley, NY: Mercury, 1996.

Zajonc, Arthur. *Meditation as Contemplative Inquiry: When
  Knowing Becomes Love*, Great Barrington, MA: Lindisfarne
  Books, 2008.

ABOUT THE AUTHOR

TORIN M. FINSER, Ph.D., is chair of the Education Department of Antioch University New England and founding member of the Center for Anthroposophy, Collaborative Leadership Training, and Templar Associates in New Hampshire. He has been an educator for three decades and has been a keynote speaker at conferences in Asia, Europe, and throughout North America. He has consulted with many public and Waldorf schools in areas of facilitating change, designing mentoring and evaluation programs, and leadership development. Dr. Finser is the General Secretary of the Anthroposophical Society in America.

As we move through our day and ponder what we see and hear, it is easy to conclude that all is not right with the world. Our foundational structures – economic, health, environmental, social – reflect a loss of humane values. Many wonder if humanity has the courage and imagination to evolve new forms.

Inspired by the work and the vision of Rudolf Steiner a century ago, anthroposophists seek to engage the better nature and higher potentials of the human being. In terms Steiner used as a young man, this involves our becoming not just knowers ("critics") or doers ("activists"), but "the one who matters most of all: the knowing doer" – the thoughtful helper, the caring researcher, the conscious human being.

Rudolf Steiner developed his own remarkable abilities into anthroposophy, or the consciousness of our humanity, a body of resources to support the healthy growth of individuals and the evolution of a humane global civilization. In the USA, the non-profit, non-sectarian Anthroposophical Society in America works to further this vision. Through more intimate personal reflection and study, group collaboration in research and community building, and devoted service to others, members try to become the change humanity needs, each according to her or his conscience and inspiration. "People must come closer to one another than they used to do," Steiner observed, "each becoming an awakener of everyone he or she meets."

To learn more, call (888.757.2742) or email us (information@anthroposophy.org) for a free copy of **being human**, our quarterly magazine.
Or read it online at **anthroposophy.org** where you can also find out more about the many faces and facets of anthroposophy today.

connecting

serving

deepening

anthroposophy.org